POP!

~~A NOVEL~~
~~A MEMOIR~~
~~A FICTIONAL MEMOIR~~
~~A NONFICTIONAL NOVEL~~
~~A FABULIST MEMOIR~~
A BOOK

BY MARK POLANZAK

stillhouse press

Fairfax, Virginia
Fall for the Book
George Mason Universtiy

Praise for Mark Polanzak's **POP!**

"Like a kaleidoscope, *POP!* turns and mixes narrative and shifts it into patterns both fluid and unpredictable. An eccentric and profound book that evokes not only our desire to remember, but our need to transform memory into story."
– Greg Hrbek, author of *Not on Fire, But Burning*

"*POP!* melds fiction and nonfiction to tell a story of loss and grief that feels so real it transcends genre labels—both a penetrating account of his father's death and an ambitious attempt to remake the memoir form. Polanzak is a fresh and energetic voice, an heir to Dave Eggers and Nick Flynn, and he's written the most innovative and engaging book I've read in ages."
– Justin St. Germain, author of *Son of a Gun*

"Finally an example of everything a twenty-first century book should be: both story and essay, entertaining and analytical, personal, ambitious, tender, outward-looking, rule-breaking, heartbreaking, funny, formally-inventive, and unlike anything I've ever read."
– Rachel Yoder, co-founder of *draft: the journal of process*

FIRST EDITION

stillhouse press

Stillhouse Press
4400 University Drive, 3E4
Fairfax, VA 22030
www.stillhousepress.org

This book does contain fictional elements, though many characters and events described by the author are real. Some characters are composites, or have been given fictitious names, while others are solely the product of the author's imagination.

Excerpts from this work originally appeared in different form in Wag's Revue and The Pinch.

Stillhouse Press is a non-profit literary organization, established in collaboration with George Mason University's Creative Writing MFA program and Northern Virginia's Fall for the Book literary festival.

Library of Congress Control Number: 2015955791
ISBN-10: 0-9905169-2-7
ISBN-13: 978-0-9905169-2-7

Art direction and cover design by Douglas J. Luman
Interior layout by Kady Dennell

Printed in the United States of America

This publisher is a proud member of

TO MA, HENRIETTA;
BRO, DAVE;
AND THE MEMORY OF DAD,
LEE POLANZAK.

CONTENTS

1 PROLOGUE ONE / **1**

2 TUESDAY morning / **7**

3 POP CULTURE / **9**

4 TUESDAY afternoon / **13**

5 PROLOGUE TWO, "PORCELAIN GOD" / **15**

6 TUESDAY afternoon / **25**

7 GRAVESITE [ongoing after] / **27**

8 GRAVE VISITS [seven and eight years after] / **29**

9 WEDNESDAY afternoon / **31**

10 DELERIUM TREMENS [47 years before] / **33**

11 WEDNESDAY afternoon / **37**

12 STARGAZER'S DISEASE [five years before and ongoing] / **39**

13 WEDNESDAY afternoon / **43**

14 TENNIS [13? 14? years before?] / **45**

15 WEDNESDAY afternoon / **47**

16 FRENZIED/SCATTERED STORY BY A MESSED UP KID,
    NEVER SHOWN TO ANYONE [four years after] / **49**
      ☺ "Arrhythmia, Arrhythmia"

17 WEDNESDAY evening / **57**

18 DENZEL WASHINGTON MOVIE [days after] / **59**

19 WRITING WORKSHOP [two years after] / **61**

20 WEDNESDAY evening / **63**

21 MOUNTAIN DEW [evolving before] / **65**

22 NAPKINS [months after] / **67**

23 WEDNESDAY evening / **71**

24 GAREWOOD, POTENTIAL FATHER [five years after] / **75**

25 GENIUS [developing without] / **79**

26 WEDNESDAY evening / **81**

27 RELIGION OVER THE POND [three weeks after] / **83**

28 THURSDAY morning / **91**

29 TRUMP CARD [one year after] / **93**

30 THURSDAY evening / **95**

31 MINI LECTURE TO MY STUDENTS
[repeatedly when I get teaching gigs] / **97**

32 THURSDAY late evening / **101**

33 FATHER'S BOOKS AND WRITINGS [five years after] / **103**

34 TENNIS [moments before] / **107**

35 GRAVE VISITS [hard to tell when but definitely after] / **111**

36 FRIDAY evening / **113**

37 PARIS [three years after] / **115**
      ☺ "The Night Before Marshall's Dad Vanished," by Marshall / **116**

38 SATURDAY morning / **121**

39 FEBRUARY 20th, 2009 [eleven years after] / **123**

40 UNRELENTING PEN PAL
[periodically and without warning after] / **125**

41 SUNDAY afternoon / **129**

42 WRITING WORKSHOP [seven years after] / **131**
      ☺ "Ready Set"

43 SAINT BUFFOON [six years before] / **135**

44 MONDAY afternoon / **137**

45 PHONES [hours after and ongoing] / **139**

46 HARMONY RUNS INTO GERTRUDE AT THE MARKET
[unknown # of years after] / **143**

47 THOUGHT AND MEMORY [always] / **149**

48 MONDAY afternoon / **151**

49 GRAVE VISITS [ten years after] / **155**

50 JUNK MAIL [some before, some after, some contemporary] / **157**

51 SWING SET UPKEEP [three years after] / **159**

52 WHAT MORRIS IS PLANNING TO DO TOMORROW
[unforeseeable future] / **161**

53 CRITIQUE / **163**

54 THE PURPOSE OF FICTION [eight years after] / **165**
      ☺ "The Man"

55 TUESDAY morning / **171**

56 "HE SUGGESTED I BURN THE MOTHER." [nine years after] / **173**

57 TUESDAY morning / **179**

58 MEETING [seven years after] / **181**

59 TUESDAY afternoon / **185**
     ☼ "Last Letters"

60 TENNIS [two years before] / **191**

61 ACES [on television] / **193**

62 HOW I IMAGINE THINGS THAT I SO VAGUELY KNOW ABOUT
   [44 years before] / **195**

63 TENNIS [in reality] / **197**

64 GRAVE VISITS [eleven years after] / **199**

65 THE NIGHTMARE AGES
   [recurring within the first few years after] / **201**

66 TUESDAY afternoon / **203**

67 OUR SECRET [before and until now] / **205**

68 TENNIS WITH HEAVEN GRAVITY [ongoing after] / **209**

69 TUESDAY evening / **211**

70 A MOMENT OF REFLECTION [as contemporary as this gets] / **221**

71 TUESDAY evening / **225**

ACKNOWLEDGMENTS / **227**
AUTHOR BIOGRAPHY / **231**

PROLOGUE ONE

POP!

Mark Polanzak's father exploded. A puff of smoke.

Mark was eating pizza with his girlfriend in the converted attic over the garage of his parents' house, when his mother collapsed into the rolling desk chair and slid a ways on the carpet, phone pressed to her right ear.

Dad's dead.

But there was no need to rush to a hospital. No need to hurry somewhere to say goodbye to a body. The body had vanished. He had exploded, just blown up during his weekly tennis match with his friends. Dr. Hutch, his doubles partner, told Mark and his mother: it was deuce point, his father's service game. Mark's dad tossed the ball up, and when he made contact, there was a dull bang as if a bottle rocket had gone off, not loud, more like a pop. A little white smoke lingered where his dad had been in the act of serving. Then, his racquet was clanging to a rest on the baseline and the ball was rolling down the net. A fault.

It shocked everyone. Nurses Mark's father had worked with, at the wake with the empty casket, they all said the same thing: "He seemed so fit, so healthy."

"Yeah," he told them. "He was young. He exercised. You never know."

Mark's brother and he had already purchased a Father's Day present. This was the second week of June, 1998. The two freshly-fatherless sons drove to the sporting goods store to return the stringing machine, but they didn't have a receipt.

"But he exploded, you see," they told the clerk.

"Store credit only."

The brothers browsed. David picked out a racquet and waved it in the air like a fly swatter; he played JV. Approaching the register, though, he hesitated. "Do you think it's safe?" he asked.

"Your game is completely different," Mark assured him.

"Yeah. I'll never have Dad's killer serve."

I'm joking, of course. No one combusts or explodes, as far as I know. This is the beginning of a fictional story I wrote. My dad did not blow up. Did not pop. He did die, though, and it wasn't funny. But I wrote this funny story about my dad's death. It goes on for many more pages, being funny and super distanced from the grief. Analogies can be drawn, though, from story to truth: the explosion and disappearance of the body reflects the unexpectedness of my father's sudden death and my never seeing the body. The line about my father being so fit intends to be humorous in the story, but that's what everyone actually did say. I didn't understand why, as if it would have been appropriate to say the opposite, if it were true: "Well, he was out of shape…" The joke about my brother's hesitation to play tennis again—as if playing tennis were the real killer—is an analogy to the fears my brother and I share that we've inherited our father's genes and will die for the reason he died: heart disease. The absurdity of returning the gift and being forced to explain that he exploded? Well, those sorts of things happen. It seems ridiculous, in real life, to explain a death in certain situations. For instance, my family had to produce a death certificate in order to change the billing information on a phone line. Who knows what crimes criminals have thought up to create such red tape? So, the ridiculousness of the story's situations isn't radically far off from the truth. It seems psycho to lose your father at seventeen. It is. The story was aiming for that. That *feeling*, I guess.

Plus, certain details are true: it was on a tennis court and during a weekly tennis date with friends that the dying occurred. However, I have no idea who had serve, whether it was Ad In or Ad Out, Deuce, or during a side change when my father's heart was attacked. What I've been told is that my dad mentioned to Dr. Hutch that he felt dizzy, then he sat on a bench to the side of the court, fainted, and his heart fluttered and fluttered. His heart began to spasm, trying to pump blood to where it needed to be. His heart tried for maybe a minute. And that was that.

An important 'however.' There was an urgent need to rush to a hospital. Dr. Hutch picked me and my mother up at the house. My girlfriend waited, too, for her mom to come and get her before Hutch arrived. How unceremonious to see her face while waiting for a trip to the hospital. She was not a bad person—a really good person actually—but just a face of ephemera, understood to soon be gone. A high school girlfriend. She was representative of a fun but passing thing in my life right in the middle of a moment that would remain. Her face is in an ever-lasting mind photo. Of destruction. My mother and I should have learned about our loss in an empty, new, and high cathedral.

My mother did say goodbye to the body. I did not. My brother did not. Dave, three thousand miles away in San Francisco, didn't even know our dad was dead yet. I was offered the chance to say goodbye. Mom promised: "He's still warm. His arms are folded on his chest like he used to sleep. I don't know how they knew he slept like that." She informed me of the state of Dad's dead body in a special room, with a couch, adjacent to the emergency room. I could hear the bigger waiting room TV through the wall. An episode of *Seinfeld* was playing.

I didn't go see the body at the wake either. A request went in to have the casket closed. At the time, I was too scared to look at my dad's dead body. Didn't know what it would do to me. I was capable of anything, I thought, and I just wanted to avoid a potential scene. However, I now think that I refused to say goodbye to my father's body because it left open the chance to find him among the living. And I want to assure you that I'm not in denial. It's been ten years since I've seen my dad, and this is because my dad is dead. But I didn't see his body, so I've allowed some part of my brain to play with the idea that my father's still out there. Maybe he escaped. Maybe he hated me and my mom and my brother and his own life. My father faked it. Disappeared. Like in the explosion story. I think about this possibility. I think that if I do clap eyes on Dad—on the subway, in some foreign city, on a someday—I'm going to clobber him.

But that is impossible.

I've never stopped inspecting strange men of my father's build, aged appropriately. I haven't stopped searching, looking, reimagining. Because my dad blew up one day, and that cannot be real.

I've written Dad's death in many ways. I've written story after story about it. I think some of them are clever. That's what writing students are supposed to do: take a real life event that has meaning and tell a story, but 'tell it slant.' So said (wrote?) Emily Dickinson, and every writing instructor reminded me of this. Emily Dickinson put all her poems in a drawer then died. She doesn't know we know her. Didn't want us to.

I want to tell you that I have been writing, taking workshops, been in writers' groups, appeared and participated in conferences, edited literary journals, written book reviews, taught creative writing courses, conducted interviews with authors, and been publishing stories of my own for the past decade now. Writing stories is all I've studied. Studied with any real dedication. This fact bothers me. One: one doesn't need formal education in writing to write a good story. Two: I've heard, said, and read so many various ideas and techniques on the subject of creative writing—many contradictory—that I have no idea what my own beliefs are anymore. Three: 'studying' writing offends people. People like my best friend's mother, who claims that one should go and live and have adventures before writing. I've always figured I've already been through an involuntary adventure. But I have chalked up more life experience in the study of writing. I learned all the tricks (which don't work), all the rules (which don't apply but here and there), all the clichés (which are alternately shit and Shinola), and I egotistically wish to banish them, to break boundaries, to prove all the teachers wrong. But I'm not going to do that. I have no idea why I'm writing instead of doing something, anything else. With this pain. Or whatever it is now. And. I want to know why. Here. In this.

I made my father's death a disappearing act: the explosion, the spontaneous combustion, and examined the absurdity of life thereafter. I drowned my dad, and told the story of becoming a lifeguard. Gave my dad cancer. Shot my dad. Drove my father's car off a cliff. Put my father in a burning building. Linked the death to a flower by the same name of the disease I killed him off with. Linked the death to idiosyncratic objects, comparing the death to little things, finding meaning in clever ways in order for the protagonist, always "Mark"—always me despite the renamings and recharacterizations— to learn just a little something about death. In the most absurd of them all, I kept my father alive and well while the protagonist grieved for not having anything to grieve about.

None of the stories do it right, though. None tell what really happened. None express how I feel.

I feel.

TUESDAY MORNING

Call me Martin, Max, Mason, Marty, Mitch, Marvin, Major, Matthew, Michael, Milo, Miles, Malcolm, Micah, Murphy, Mo, Morris, Manny, Marshall, Mitchell, and Mark. I do.

My mother mentions a bereavement group. That she is attending? That she is somethinging. There is a bereavement group meeting in a community center somewhere. It meets somewhere regularly. Maybe it meets in a church basement. Mom mentions it. She mentions me coming. Talking there? Who knows what exactly she is doing. What she knows. How she is communicating it to me. We are on the phone. It's a tertiary act while frying eggs or reading over edits or thinking about something else or finding an ashtray. Staring off. Just saying yeah. There is a pattern to these conversations with my mom. Somewhere in her speaking is the word *appointment* or *activity*. There is an obligation with a date and time attached, maybe even a location. *Doctor. Dentist. Play downtown. Museum exhibition. Open studio. Help at the house. Someone needs help moving. Wedding. Funeral. Lunch.* My role is to say yeah and wait for the date to pass. This is the way of it. She knows it and doesn't appear to mind; she doesn't want to do the things she is asking me to participate in any more than I do. It works out well for the two of us. She likes making plans. Not doing them. She may even use me as an excuse just when she's scheduled to head out the door.

I am not working that much, underemployed, having recently quit the bar bouncing, the midmorning to afternoon bartending, and English tutoring gigs. I should be searching for new gigs. I have nowhere to be. Almost ever. I held onto the creative writing workshops at the Adult Education Center in Boston. But essentially an unstructured life, so I make plans with myself to write, to edit, or to read. A fellowship without having to have won it—just underemployed and under-motivated to find work. Not having a job, not having any obligations but to oneself has its drawbacks. I can't tell anyone that I am 'busy' and can't say 'no' to anyone's demands on my time. *What are you doing that is so important?* So, I say yeah to my mom. Say yes to something I don't understand, something I don't really hear. I flip the eggs out of the pan, underline the sentence to rewrite, snuff out the cigarette. Hang up. Almost totally forget the thing.

But the word *bereavement* is part of what I agreed to. And *group* and *meeting*. Somewhere in Massachusetts. This is what I remember for a minute here.

Wait a second! Is Mom attending a bereavement group now? Now? After ten years? Have I been checking in on her enough? She must not be attending. Someone told her about it. Some bereft so-and-so told her to just come by or stop in. Mom's going along to this meeting in order to morally support someone who actually needs this type of group. That's it. She's doing a favor for this someone. And she wants me to accompany her accompanying, I guess. I feel. I satisfy myself.

Wait for the date to pass.

POP CULTURE

It's scattershot. This stuff. We go over here. We go over there. We move forward. We get knocked back. In the middle of a normal Tuesday, something pops up, and we are thrown for a loop. We pick ourselves up, we dust ourselves off. Then we get turned upside down. We roll with the punches, then throw one of our own. We find ourselves in a job, in a relationship, and we ponder it maybe for a moment. How did we get here? Then something gets remembered. Something gets imagined. We say we want to live in the moment. We say that actually we have to plan for the future. We say that the past is the past. We say that the past is prelude. We say that the past must not be forgotten. We say the past is history. Spirits rise tonight. Trick or treat, we say. A firecracker goes POP. Fall into Winter. We say the future looks bright. We say tomorrow will be better. We say our future is doomed. We say the present is a constantly evolving past. We forget something, then we remember it wrong. We say that's not the way it happened, no. We say, I can't remember. We say, oh yeah, that's it! We say that was before I, that was after we, that was right at the time that you, that was when we. We tell lies. We admit to telling lies. We lie to get to tomorrow. We are honest about the past when it's past. We say, all that matters is now. We hope for the best and prepare for the worst. We say, next time we'll know what to do. We say, if that ever happens again. We say, lesson learned. We say never again. We revise. We edit. We get it right. Then something pops up. We want the children to be the future. Our parents, the past. We say, we are in the prime of our lives. Everything is going to turn around today. Things are looking up. Peaks and valleys, we say. We say thank god for rollercoasters or we'd not know how to describe this life. We say, sleep on it. See how we feel in the morning. Put it to bed. Don't borrow trouble. No use crying. Give up the ghost. We say enjoy it while we can. Have a cigar. Have a glass of champagne. We say Happy New Year. A confetti gun goes POP. We say it's a clean slate. We say this year we will. We resolve to. We say no regrets. We say we're sorry. We quit this. We take up that. We quit that. We say that was a phase. This is a fad. We say another go round. We say there's only one ride. We say legacy. Monument. Memorial. We say dust to dust. We say Winter into Spring. Anniversary, we say. A champagne cork goes POP. We say Tuesday into Wednesday. We say hump day. We say halfway done. We say halfway started. We want the best for you. Best for us, too. We want to help out. We say we're getting better at asking for help. Teamwork, we say. We say individual. We say this is your life! We say that when we were little we wanted to be. We say pipe dreams. Delusions of grandeur. We say sidetracked. Backtracked. Derailed. We say we're en route. Be there shortly. We say we have a headache. Stomachache. We say we need to soul search. We say pursuit. Passion. Duty. Obsession. Hobby. Chore. We say we do it all for you. We say we won't really do it if it isn't for ourselves first and foremost. We say tomorrow. Next week. Next year. Next time. We say accomplished. We say on to a new goal. We see a psychic. Psychologist. Psychiatrist. Life coach. Friend. Parent. Brother. Sister. We need divine intervention. We say malarkey. We say top of the Eiffel tower. Back to nature. We can't go home again. We say congratulations. Hooray! We give our condolences. Our prayers are with you. You are in our thoughts. We say anything you need. We say don't trouble yourself. We say we're here for you. We say back in fifteen minutes. We say reunion. We say divorce. We say for the children. We say for the best. We say happy Fourth of July! A bottle rocket goes POP. We say for our founding fathers. We say give us your poor and sickly. We say every man. We see fire in the sky. We see colors where they shouldn't be. We gather in fields, on harbors, along beaches, on folding chairs, on blankets, lying on grass, on sand, on your chest. We look up. We say ooo. We say ahhh. We are illuminated. The sky is bright at night. We listen to the booms. We hear bang. We are just fine right here, right now, for once. We say come closer to us. We say hold our hand. We say we love you. Don't you know that? Something goes POP.

TUESDAY AFTERNOON

And it's October again. Significance: little, save for an unexplained and recurring dive bomb into depression. I can explain June's, or the first two weeks of June. I can explain the torpor brought on by Boston's late February snow prison, like anyone else. But I'm not sure about October's brand of funk. Still, I expect it to come and hope to sneak out of the month quickly, quietly. Get into November. Come up for air. And turkey. Who knows? Presidential debates rage on flat screens—Obama and the other guy. It's still warm enough to smoke morning cigarettes and drink morning coffees (Marlboro Mediums, French Press) on the roof out my window. View: little.

I've just moved into a studio apartment in Cambridge. Cambridgeport is the specific area. I'm still making frequent trips to Target and furniture shops around town. Buying plants because I've seen them in other people's apartments. Buying melon ballers that I hope to someday have use for. Replacing dead plants.

Citizens of Cambridge are called Cantabridgians. Does that make any sense?

How to make one's day valuable when not working 40 hours a week? Brand yourself a writer, I guess. That's what I did. Go to the laptop. The Moleskin. Feel good with the coffee or wine or Miller. Light up a smoke. Open up Word. Look at what you've got going on. You are contributing to the world with this stuff! Eh.

I've set up the 'speech' tool in Word. I highlight one of my stories in progress. Tell the computer to read my story to me. Kick back. Bask in my own words. Sip coffee. Blow smoke rings out the skylight. See what needs revising, reworking in the fiction.

No plans in the foreseeable future. No meetings. Nothing to prepare for. Nothing but the rest of my life on the horizon.

PROLOGUE TWO

"PORCELAIN GOD"

The dudes who remodeled my mom's master bathroom forgot to take away the old pink toilet. So there it stood, in the middle of our front yard—a constant amidst the turning, falling leaves of autumn.

We figured they'd be back for it, the toilet. After a week or so of rousing suspicion among the other residents of Green Street, the unspoken realization hit us: that pink throne was our problem now.

One crisp November afternoon, my mom and brother and I all found ourselves standing around the thing with steaming cups of coffee in our hands. My mug had a chip and read: "Nobody's Perfect."

"How heavy is it?" My brother tried his best to surmise the toilet's heft with his mind then tilted it with his free hand.

"Don't hurt yourself," cautioned my mother.

"Well?" I wanted to hear that it was no problem; that Devon would throw it on his back and carry it to wherever hoppers go to rest in peace.

"Like a boulder," he said, sliding a timid step back from it, sipping his coffee.

We just stared at the thing for a while, in silence. A leaf landed on it. We eyed each other.

Later on, we were back in separate rooms of the house, all of us pretty sure that that toilet situation would just take care of itself.

If my dad hadn't gone and had a heart attack and died during a tennis date last winter, we would have let him deal with the throne's removal. It was his after all. Well, we all conducted business with it, over the years, the taco nights. But my dad, he used it exclusively, never settling for a leak in the downstairs half bath, or maybe just a gassy false alarm in the upstairs hall john. The rest of us were equal opportunity with our ones and twos.

The only time I saw my father naked, he was draining the lizard into that pink toilet. He was upset, I remember. I was little; I flung open the door and froze. My old man looked up; he sighed; he breathed my name. He was never angry before or after that. Something cosmic transpired between my dad and the pink toilet that my encroaching upon disrupted. Also, outside that moment, I never saw him vulnerable. Except, of course, he was vulnerable and probably pretty pissed when his heart went and dropped the ball at deuce point.

Besides the toilet on the lawn, there were other new features at the Paterson household. For one, my brother was there all the time. He bailed on his life across the country, in San Francisco, after Dad bailed on his for good. When December rolled around, Devon began to pick up the pieces, got a marketing gig in Beantown, started saving for an apartment. I was in my senior year at a ridiculous private school, applying to ridiculous colleges. California schools looked good junior year, but I narrowed the list to campuses within driving distance to our house, to our pink toilet. Mom, despite talking vaguely of renewing her RN credits, stayed locked away in her room more and more. When I returned from school, she would be wrapped in her red and black flannel robe, in bed watching bad *Lifetime* movies, or at the computer googling involved French recipes that I certainly never had the pleasure of eating.

We were curious when the first snowfall began covering the pink toilet—would the thing go out of sight, out of mind? Early one morning, the first flakes made a white and pink polka-dotted sculpture of the toilet in our yard.

"Shit," shouted my brother, and I hadn't sensed that he was standing behind me, watching through the window, too. "We need to take a picture." He ran off, then appeared in the yard with his camera, motioning for me to come out, and mouthing *bring the paper*. I grabbed the Sunday Globe and trotted down the steps.

We met up at the toilet.

"Sit on it," he said.

"On the toilet?"

"Like you're taking a shit."

I lifted the seat.

"Don't actually crap in the thing. Just sit on the lid."

I did so.

"Now read the paper." Devon danced around and snapped photos from all angles. At first, he was framing the shots for whole minutes, preserving the moment, the image, me on the toilet. He looked so focused, like he was staring at a developing cure in his Petri dish, Petri crapper. All of a sudden, I wanted to try and deal with it like my brother; I got into the whole charade. I mimed unzipping and fire hosing it. I pretended to barf, praying to the porcelain God. I laughed. My bro laughed. I faked all embarrassed like getting barged in on. Posing for a swirly proved too difficult. When we were through, Devon out of film, I depressed the handle, folded the paper under my arm, and whistled my way back inside with Devon chuckling and winding his camera behind me.

At the new toilet, relieving myself of what all the pretend bathroom business had conjured, I thought, so that's how it happens, that's how people wind up with junk on display around their property. Something is kind of too heavy or annoying to remove, then you get attached to it. It was sad and scary that though my dad was a doctor and I was in private school, none of that matters when you've got a toilet in your front yard. Presto—White Trash.

It was a white Christmas that year, first in a decade we were told. Mom said we were too grown-up to get presents, to get a tree, to put up the little white lights, and we agreed; I still didn't know or care exactly what a Yule log was. I didn't want any gifts anyhow, at least nothing that she could have given me. We gave Mom a nosegay of daisies and yellow roses though, and, of course, she cried, and Christmas was saved only when Devon rolled up an eternally constipated snowman to sit on the snowtoilet. He called Mom out to see, and she laughed. When she laughed, it was good. I watched through the window, her breath a misty cloud, then gone. The snowman strained. It was good for her and for Devon.

After New Year's, a new orange bottle fluttered into existence on the white laminate countertop of our kitchen. Mom called them her happy pills. She didn't seem to be taking the proper amount at first. It is slightly more upsetting, I noticed, to have someone around who is too happy rather than too sad, especially when you know they're manufactured smiles. Either way, throughout that winter, Mom was out of bed before me, with breakfast made and everything.

"Am I doing an OK job with you, sweetie?" she asked, over scrambled eggs and coffee.

"Of course, mom. You're the best." I didn't look up.

"Good. I'm so proud of you, you know."

"I know."

"Dad is proud of you, too."

Pregnant pause.

"You can talk to him, you know." She brushed my hair back with the tips of her fingers. My head, a block of ice.

Along with my mother's newfound energy came a confusing and weird spirituality. This involved, as far as I could tell, a mixture of referring to Dad as still *with us* and watching the *X Files*. After an episode in which the ghost of a little girl keeps appearing to her mother, and the ghost-girl helps solve her own murder, my mother declared: "I believe that." I told her to hang a shingle, do some readings.

One night, my eyes popped open, awoken by what I thought to be, please God, a scantily clad and thieving nymph. Out in the yard, under the gently falling flakes, in her pale blue nightgown, my mother stared intently at the pink toilet, part of which had peeked out from the snow. The silver handle glowed in the spotlight of the full moon. I stood next to my mom in my boxers and slippers, glancing at her, then the toilet, then her. Her eyes were bright and fixed on the thing. She smiled a calm and all-knowing little smile, and a tear rolled down her moon white cheek. I put my shivering hand on her warm and steady shoulder.

"Sweetie?" she whispered. "Did you hear it flush too?"

Devon moved into his new pad in the Fens that February. His bathroom had a claw foot tub and a red hopper. "Close but no TP roll," he said, indicating the thing. He developed and framed all his toilet art, and they were the first things to go up. Beautiful black and white and vivid color. Some shots of leaves swirling about the thing went in the kitchen. Some of the thing half encased in snow went in the hall. One with me reading the paper went in the bathroom. He hung with care. The one picture of the toilet in a lightning storm went in his bedroom. Last, he placed an ancient photograph of us, the smiling family, on his nightstand.

"So, that's how important we are," I said, looking from the tiny ancient guy to the gallery of pink toilets.

"Nothing matters more. Come here." Devon must have misheard, since he was spreading his arms for a hug.

God, my girlfriend sucked. Of course, she was on student government. Of course, she was an A student at a ridiculously competitive private school. Of course, she was pretty and happy. Of course, she sang in the a capella group. Of course, somehow, she knew how not to look like an idiot while dancing. Of course, she was involved in the theater department while balancing her commitments to softball and field hockey. Of course, she founded the all-female anglers society. Of course, she was a freshman mentor. And of course, she sucked.

When she marched around the corner into Gleason hall, where I was enjoying a doughnut, during one of my free periods, I just knew that she wanted me to *do something*. And not anything useful, like make out in the music rooms, but be productive or whatever, *participate*.

She smiled her hey-I-seem-to-have-too-many-teeth smile and waved an I'm-so-excited-to-see-that-you're-not-busy wave, which, frankly, I didn't agree with. The doughnut. She sat down and flung off her gargantuan purple backpack.

"Baby," she said, and it didn't sound sweet; it was a serious, business "baby." "There's a freshman boy whose father..." She trailed off, sliding her eyes around like fishing lures. "His father *passed on*."

"Bought the farm. Checked out. Kicked the bucket. Ate his last doughnut." I shouted them out while she cast treble hooks through me. "It's *died*, baby." I employed the business-baby, too.

"Fine. His father *died*. Anyway, I told Mr. Sweat that you'd talk with him if he needed to talk, and apparently, the boy wants to talk. Can you talk?" She grabbed my free hand.

"Mr. Sweat's first name. Is it Richard?"

"What?"

It took her a second, but when she got it, I was almost in love again. Soon enough though, she was mad at me like always: telling me that she was no longer asking, that I don't do anything anyhow, that I'm always hanging around after school, that I'm avoiding activities and home, that I haven't been to any club meetings in months, that the boy's name isn't Dick either, and that I had to meet him after classes, in the bio wing. Then, she was gone, off to her million other obligations, me being one that she was sucking at.

"This doughnut tastes bitter. And where's that side of betrayal I ordered?" No one else was free that period to hear my quips.

So, I found myself in the bio wing, surrounded by standing plastic skeletons, deconstructable mockups of human hearts and human brains, and big maps of the human body with red and blue veins squeezing pink striated muscle tissue. I was studying the urethra and bladder when I heard the kid.

"You Martin," the kid said.

"You the kid whose father *passed on*?"

He didn't respond. He just stood there, in the doorway, looking down and kicking at the checkered black and white linoleum with his bucks.

"You got a mom?" I asked.

He nodded.

"Brothers? Sisters?"

"Older brother."

"Man, do we have a lot in common. I got a mom, an older brother, and, of course, the dead dad. I got it all!"

The kid went and sat down at a big black table with Bunsen burners all over it. I sat behind the teacher's desk, spun a metal replica of an atom, then folded my hands.

"How's it been?" I wanted to hear that it was nothing at all; that this kid would just throw his sadness on his back and carry it off to wherever you take sadness.

"I hate everybody and everything."

No dice. "How'd it go down?"

"Cancer."

"Lungs? Muscle? Ear?"

"Brain." He fiddled with a Bunsen burner.

"Brain. Heart." I held up a piece of hippocampus and a left ventricle. "Both major players in the body. Both hugely important to human survival." I juggled the bits of organ along with a rubber large intestine. "Slow death. Surprise death. Still dead. We all bought a ticket, kid: a one-way ticket to the bone yard."

The kid just sat there, in his required school tie, looking down, looking scared. He was coming to me. Boy, was he lost, this kid, who was about to torch himself on the Bunsen burner because he was now a zombie. Just going through the motions. And why shouldn't he be sad? Why shouldn't he be scared? He obviously has no idea how to deal with having his life all flipped around and slammed in the toilet. Then flushed. Then plunged. He didn't expect that. He didn't deserve that. Just a kid who got robbed.

Then, something miraculous happened. Someone, something, some god spoke through me. "Everyone finds some way to deal with a loss. My brother, for example, he has busied himself with a job, a goal, and has been doing his best to laugh at memories of his father. My mother, after losing her husband, she has sought some medical help, developed a connection to a power greater than herself, and she is essentially making it now. And they've done this on their own, found these solaces. Truth is, kid, this is kind of an individual thing, this coping with loss. There's no right way. And no one can help you find your way. Everyone has his or her own technique, method, or process. You can try to do what others do. You can observe what your mother does, but maybe it's not your way. Perhaps, for you, it will not come quickly, but listen: it will come. Try to believe: it will come." When I escaped my trance, it was just me and the fake human parts left in the room. I put my hand on a skeleton's shoulder. He wobbled.

That spring, when snow melted off branches, revealing oaks and maples; when icicles slipped from gutters and basketball nets; when grass rippled out in soccer fields and birds sang again, so, too, did the pink toilet bloom, emerging from its icy hibernation.

Everything would burn bright green that summer: the leaves, the blades of grass, the ponds deep in the woods. Devon would take a stroll in the common with a new girlfriend, who worked as a biomedical engineer, and he would be fascinated by the fact that she wore a lab coat and worked on curing diseases. Mom would renew her RN credits, start part time at Mass General. She would make a meal that had frogs' legs. They would both come with me to Accepted Candidates Day at college and marvel at all the buildings and opportunities. My girlfriend would win several awards at graduation, wear special neon tassels, and lie to me, saying that she was most proud of our relationship. I would break up with her as soon as I got to school in the fall. I would meet girls that didn't ask anything of me, but just wanted to get drunk and it on. I would bump a lot of speed. I would steal a golf cart from campus security, park it on the stage of the auditorium, and I wouldn't be caught for this. I would get by, majoring in business, and I would move close to my mother and brother after getting my BS. We would watch the Red Sox with new girlfriends. Mom would bring us good food to our apartments. She would meet another doctor, and he would treat her well and never make me or Devon feel weird. Devon would have a baby before I did, and he would name him after our dad. I would be his godfather and make jokes about the mafia. There would be new houses purchased. There would be new graduations to attend. There would be laughs, and there would be cries. There would be a world, and it would spin lazily through a black void.

And the pink toilet would grow pipes, roots into the soil of our front yard. Tall grass would grow up around it. Mom would place nosegays of daisies and yellow roses in its basin, a good planter. The pink toilet would be there every time I returned to my childhood home. My wife would joke that she needed to pee so bad that she'd use the pink one. Our Christmas photos would be taken around the pink throne. Thanksgiving cigars would be smoked around it.

Somehow, the pink toilet would look beautiful and good in our front yard, after years and years and years. Most of the time though, we'd be too busy or far away to think about the pink toilet. And it would wait, through wind and rain and snow and lightning for us to remember. Everyone and everything would live long and happy and healthy. The toilet would live forever and ever in our yard. In our hearts.

Pink throne.

Porcelain God.

STUPID. FUCKING. THING.

TUESDAY AFTERNOON

My computer finishes the reading. I'm plucking a Telecaster my dad gave me by the end of the story.

My father was a doctor, an anesthesiologist, yes. I was at a ridiculously exclusive and expensive private school, yes. My brother did move from San Francisco back to the Boston area and lived in an apartment near Fenway, yes. And we did in fact have a pink toilet that the dudes forgot to take away, yes. However, the toilet never wound up in the yard, and my father never used it. The pink toilet was in the "second floor hall John." The only toilet that my father even acknowledged was in the master bathroom, which was in fact lime green and never got remodeled. The toilet is in my mom's garage to this day, and none of us give a damn about it. It has no meaning, except in the story. In life, it's just a toilet. My brother did mention wanting to place the toilet in the yard after reading the story. He felt we could ascribe new meaning to it. He was chuckling when he suggested this. I don't know how I feel about it.

The *shitty* truth behind this story is that I wrote it with so many external devices in my head that, to me, it is essentially bloodless. Maybe I pulled the wool in others' readings. But. Here's how the piece came to be: My writing-school poet-friend read me the Beckett story "Dante and the Lobster" in his amazing, crummy apartment in the desert with its blue cement floors during one of our chess nights, which many times devolved into drinking too many beers and reading stories and poems. I lost a critical mass of those matches. I immediately wanted to write a story with a final line like the one in the Beckett story: *"It is not."* As powerful as it is strong; as funny as it is humorous; as weird as it is odd! That last line shows an authorial hand slamming down and declaring a truth from some godlike point of view. The story's about a day in Dublin in which the viewpoint character reads some Dante, then makes lunch, then buys a lobster, then comes home to his aunt's house to cook the lobster. When the VC realizes that this lobster lived its life, made its love, battled its peril, and survived the wild ocean simply to be boiled here and now in his aunt's kitchen, our VC hesitates to take the lobster's life. His aunt mollifies our VC, explaining that the lobster's death will be a quick one. "It is not," unmollifies Beckett, explaining to the reader that life and death are painful and long. I don't feel that bad about starting my own story with the hope of emulating a master or due to a specific artistic inspiration from a master, because Beckett was copying Joyce. What does concern me about my own story is that it is formulaic. The idea of the story is to link a super Big Life Experience (DEATH!) to something small and seemingly meaningless (toilet). It works. The two get linked, and the symbol of the story is ironic and used to show how this family reacted to death by reacting instead, base-artfully, to a toilet. That's craft. It's all craft. When you can see craft in a story, something's way more than wrong. And the end, with the shouting and swearing? That's way off, because I wasn't angry at seventeen. I was nothing at seventeen. I was a zombie, of course. So, that's wrong. The idea is a formula. The inspiration is someone else's story. And the feeling is inaccurate, I think. Actually, the protagonist never says how he feels. That's the problem.

I will do it, though. It is my goal to express it the right way. I've gone looking for a way to tell this story everywhere, which is a reworked line from a Denis Johnson story.

My dad's spirit lies not in a magical toilet.

Onward.

GRAVESITE

[ONGOING AFTER]

Marvin's father's grave, which is a plaque in the ground, not a tombstone, reads: "Mitchell Lee Polanzak, M. D." This is inaccurate information, misleading to the casual viewer of this particular Forever Spot. His father's real name was (is?): Mitchell Leo Polanzak. So, when Marvin and his mother and brother were in the cemetery's office, selecting the grave design, debating between a floral or tennis-racquetal border, they made a mistake. It's a lie. The grave lies. His middle name was (is?): Leo, not Lee. His death certificate doesn't match his birth certificate. However, this permanent lie is more to the truth, because Marvin's dad went by Lee. Never once did Marvin hear anyone call him Mitchell. Not once, Leo. His name was Lee. What the grave should say, lying yet harder, is "Lee Polanzak." Or to Marvin's mind, "Dad." But. That's what's on his grave, a revision of the truth. A fiction. But more truthful.

The "M. D." is also wrong. He was a doctor. But he never asked anyone to address him as Doctor Polanzak. He was first a father and husband. He was second a tennis player. Marvin doesn't even know how far down the identifying-stuff-list Dad would put his medical background. A PhD once introduced himself as doctor so-and-so to his father, and Marvin waited, knowing what Dad would say in response, proud as hell at the man's whatever-it-was (is?): "I'm Lee," he said. But they, those who survived, put that "M. D." down there in the ground. They were proud he was a doctor. This is a truth on his grave that represents reality, not perception, which is all the reality one has.

It's all getting mixed up quick, isn't it?

GRAVE VISITS

[SEVEN AND EIGHT YEARS AFTER]

"The thing that really gets me, that really hurts, that is really fucked up about this? She is the only person I've ever taken to Dad's grave." Dean is telling Micah about how Daisy has broken up with him yet again. "I took her there. I trusted her. I—" He gets too mad, too something, to finish his thought.

Micah just listens. He has opinions that are going to bias him. He loves his brother. The two are on opposite sides of the country. Dean in Los Angeles. Micah on Martha's Vineyard. How many bodies of water separate the two brothers? The Atlantic, the Cape Cod Channel. The Connecticut River? The Mississippi, of course. A great lake. The two brothers are far away from each other, and Micah loves Dean, and he wants to destroy everything that hurts Dean, which, in this instant, is Daisy. He wants her dead.

"We went there. Me and Daisy. And we sat for, I don't know. We sat there. We lay there, in front of Dad's grave. Right there with him. I put my head in her lap. She touched my head. I cried. She cried. We went there. I thought it was safe. I thought I could trust her. *Why did I take her?*"

Not: *why did she break up with me.*

"That's OK, Dean. That's OK. That is for you, not for her. That place is for you, you can't taint it."

But Micah knows he himself has tarnished the sacred spot.

Micah took one of his girlfriends to Dad's grave, too. He wanted to show her him. Really him. It was a sham. Because he never feels anything when he goes to the grave. Every time, he touches the grave, wipes away leaves, chunks of mowed grass to reveal the misprinted name down there. He does this slowly—with respect for what, he doesn't know. But he took her there under false pretenses. They were to share in something very special, but it wasn't going to be special, at least for Micah. Bereavement is his bag, and he uses it in this wrong way. Bringing her there. It was an easy way to show a depth in him that is fraudulent, because he's never actually honestly felt something and expressed it appropriately.

Sitting there, on the grass on a beautiful day with her, he forced out a cry. A fake little cry—an actor's cry. He hoped it gave him impunity with the girl, gave him a full commitment from her.

But they broke up eventually, too. Micah never called Dean to share the same sad story of her being the only one he took to the grave, but he could have. But he didn't have the same pain as Dean about it. A different pain. A pain of not seeing the place as dear and special. He didn't feel anything there. With the right girl, with real security and love, Micah will be able to say the truth at the grave: "I don't know what I'm supposed to do here. Is that weird?"

WEDNESDAY AFTERNOON

We broke up. Anna and me. Couple months ago. Got back together though. Couple months ago. I am having a new apartment, you see. Anna is the first girlfriend I've lived with. We started September of last year and lasted until this past summer. She got the apartment in the trial separation. I got a new attic studio. But we're reimagining our relationship as together but separate. We don't fit together, but I crave commitment. This week, she's finally moving out and on from our shared place.

I come to inside my old apartment. Where she and I lived and fought. Everything's in boxes. I don't miss this place—the anonymous granite countertop, the cold stainless steel everywhere, the slippery hardwood floors—or Anna's stuff—the precious picture frames and heirlooms in the old-money display cabinet, her one thousand thread count taste. I won't miss our cohabitation, but I do hate the feeling of failure, a fucked up opportunity I might've had at forging a new home, with new family members.

I plan on mentioning my mom's new group to see if she can piece it together. Anna's sitting cross-legged on her faded pink and yellow striped area rug that she placed under her unfinished narrow rough-cut wood coffee table. She's in navy blue sweat pants and a white tank top. She's got trinkets in her lap. Love's like a lap—it's certainly always a part of you, always there, but you got to create it. You can't run.

"Remember this place?" she asks.

And I hate this place and want nothing but to forget it.

"Yeah." But it's totally different. I'm lost in here today. "Where's the uh—" I make stabbing motions with my hand.

"In here." She points at the ceiling.

She's leaving, too. Her parents bought her a condo on the other side of town. She's remodeling the whole thing. Make a new nowhere. Another not mine. Not hers. Another on-deck circle. It must be crummy to be so well off that you never get the chance to earn anything, build something. I never get the chance to do my mentioning of my mentionable thing.

I'm drawing open drawers, crawling in closets, stepping on stairs, running in rooms, chanting up the chimney, backing into boxes, crouching behind couches, ripping up rags, scanning over scraps, traveling out of time, searching through so many somethings. For what?

"Where's the uh—"

DELERIUM TREMENS

[47 YEARS BEFORE]

Miles is reading poetry in his studio apartment in Cambridgeport. There are others who have written their dads' deaths.

Thomas's father, Shaw, taught literature at a grammar school nearer to the beginning of the twentieth century. Strict was his demeanor in the classroom, for he had known, within himself, that his intelligence, ability to comprehend words and impart knowledge far exceeded the confines of the grammar school. Shaw believed, like so many of us, that he was unrewarded for a thing that existed within only his mind.

But if you caught Shaw not meditating on how the world had left the stone over his head unturned, if he was not remembering at a particular moment that he *deserved*, then you could hear his laugh, a great Ka-BOOM!

And that's how he lived. Though, he did have an exceptional son. Special for a reason. Poetry.

Unsuddenly, over one period of time, Shaw's health declined: his taut forearms sagged; his rosy cheeks paled; his laugh coughified. He became weak. Gentle.

Now, Shaw's son, Thomas, grew up to be much the same as his father, at least physically. If a discrepancy in their intelligence existed—maybe more, maybe same?—it was no matter. Luck, might it have been, favored Thomas's career more than Shaw's, to be sure. Thomas's reaction to his father's decline and impending death was complicated. He was disappointed, it seemed. In a poem for his father, Thomas demanded that his father: "Rage against the dying of the light" and to "not go gentle into that good night." Thomas wanted his father's Ka-BOOM to explode on.

If this were one of Miles's stories and not a flowery summation of the death of Dylan Thomas' father, he would have no idea what to say next. You see, Thomas was there to watch his father die and knew it was coming. The loss obviously affected Thomas. It inspired or conjured or created his most well known poem: "Do not go gentle into that good night." In a story of Miles's, most likely the crux would be something utterly moot in the actual lives of the two men: the struggle with putting into words the death of his father; or the poet's evolving battle with truly feeling something rather than writing about it or Thomas's desire to one-up his father. Something American. These American feelings, by all accounts, were not Thomas's drive.

The death poem is a villanelle. A poetic form in which two rhymed lines repeat throughout, appearing in the last line of each stanza, alternating. It is a strict form—rigid, old. Thomas had nothing to do with the form's invention. There was nothing new about this approach at all. Curious. Why borrow a form, why take something off the shelf in which to encase your singular experience? Perhaps, Thomas knew there was nothing new about this experience. Death happens everywhere, always. Moreover, the poem was published almost immediately. Was Thomas simply exploiting his pain for a good couple lines and a credit? Is not the death of a loved one, especially your father, for private consumption? Maybe Thomas was declaring that his personal loss was, in fact, a public one—that with the death of every single human, we all, all of us lose together?

Miles, in the quiet of his apartment with a notebook and pen imagines that Thomas visited his father in the hospital one night, regarded his father's weakened state, saw the decay, and was mixed up about it: sad, angry, hopeful. Possibly. Not a wild conjecture on Miles's part. But, he imagines on—to Thomas's drive home, to his jingling pocket change walking up to the front door of his house, looking down, noticing and not noticing cracks in the concrete, the quiet of the moment registered through the clarity of tiny specific sounds.

He imagines the poet went right to his notebook and began writing. And that writing session which produced "Do not go gentle..." had nothing to do with death or poetic form or his father. It had to do with a general loneliness of a moment that is always there when he writes. For a moment Loneliness was almost strong enough to manifest, to move a pencil. To talk.

Thomas's father's death is famous.

No one knows just how Thomas himself died, but Miles's heard this about that: Thomas sat at a bar in New York, The White Horse. He drank all day, he drank and drank until he fell into a coma.

Way to not go gentle. Way to rage.

Miles drinks from a brown bottle and turns up the music.

WEDNESDAY AFTERNOON

I pack a few boxes at Anna's place, our old place. She hasn't prepared well and has been ordered by the landlord (her brother-in-law) to be out of here by tomorrow morning. The apartment is soon to be inhabited by another couple whose fate is also indeterminable. I feel like a kid in some sort of adult game.

I've never helped a girl pack up and move who has prepared properly, who has realized that there are—in any given apartment or house even tent—approximately ten more boxes of stuff behind cupboards, in drawers, crammed in closets, hidden in the walls than you're expecting. So, I do my part—look annoyed and put nose down—then head to the commuter train to visit my mother out in the burbs. Another chore. Another thing to check off an imaginary 'to-do list' of my current unscheduled life.

I can't see well enough to read the train tracks and times. I hear the numbers flipping over, clacking on the big board in the center of South Station, but it's no use. I have learned that a voice announces which train, making which stops, is boarding on which track. This happens roughly ten to eight minutes before the train's scheduled departure. I listen to announcements for train departures and tracks that are for other people to worry about, twenty minutes before mine is to take off. Obviously, there's quite a din in this major hub of transportation in Boston. The room is all glass and steel and stone and clocks and change falling out of pockets and birds flying through and babies and ordering food and doors slamming and loud headphones and thoughts. This makes the announcement choppy, as audible as a friend at a rock show or an alien transmission, come 40 million light years. I locate the spot inside South Station with the best announcement volume, a triangulation in between a group of speakers that do the broadcasting from fifty feet up in the rafters. I close my eyes. I strain.

STARGAZER'S DISEASE

[FIVE YEARS BEFORE AND ONGOING]

Before Marty's dad died, there was a chance, for a month or so, that he would die first.

All of a sudden Marty couldn't see right. One day he was sitting in the back row of the classroom, note-taking from the chalkboard up there at the front, passing notes to friends at a safe distance from the teacher's eyes. The next day, he was somewhere in the middle of the room, squinting, although squinting accomplished very little. Soon enough, Marty was in the first row and couldn't read the damn words on the board.

Mom and Dad were informed by lab-coated men that there was more than a small chance that their son had a tumor right behind his gray eyes.

Marty was what? Twelve? Thirteen? when this all went down? Some of the sights, sounds, smells, touches, and tastes of the events that followed the tentative diagnosis are not going to leave him until he gets his fair share of dementia down the road.

The maybe-brain tumor took Marty on his first subway ride in Boston. Marty, Mom, and Dad were underground, on a packed Orange line train, headed to the Mass Eye and Ear Clinic. Marty remembers precisely where they were going because he has recently seen the Mass Eye and Ear Clinic and finally figured out that they were not, in fact, back then, headed to the Messiah-Near Clinic on his first subway ride. What great names for horrible places! They visited the Floating Hospital, which delighted Marty's mind—he wanted it to actually be a ship, but it's just a concrete slab with sick people trying to get well and healthy people trying to get them well. They visited Children's Hospital, which he had hoped looked exactly the same as a regular hospital but was staffed entirely by elementary schoolers running all over with stethoscopes around their necks. Mass General, which Marty thought was the exact center of the galaxy, wherefrom all matter emitted.

A test: stick your head here, then we'll enclose it with a white globe. We'll put straps on your neck, so you won't move your head. Hold this clicker. Now click when you see a tiny white-hot dot of light move into your field of vision. Do this for, I don't know, an hour?

A test: Here, give me your arm. Inside this hypodermic needle you will find a fluid that lights up your insides like toxic sewage. You will vomit on the floor right here in the office. We'll clean it. You'll vomit again. You'll be super confused. Now get in this tube. Stay there for, I don't know, an hour?

A bonus: when you go home, pee. Your pee is going to look fucking awesome. Call your family in for them to see this hyper orange, otherworldly pee, but don't expect Mom or Dad to enjoy it (you won't know this, but it reminds them that you are being tested for cancer or an abhorrent eye disease). Your brother won't care at all. He'll tell you it's gross, because he doesn't know what's going on. He's listening to a lot of Nirvana and Pearl Jam right now, and would really appreciate it if you all just chilled and left him alone, all right? But you two aren't close yet. You will be after Dad dies, though. In a weird way. Then, in a good way.

A meeting:

The doctor was fat and bald and the windowless room was dark, lit by a few small desk lamps, not like a doctor's office at all. Marty was in the special chair in the middle of the room, parents behind him, in less special chairs, and the doctor wheeling around in front in a slightly special chair. The doc was telling it straight.

"What do you want to be when you grow up, Marty?" he asked.

"A radiologist," Marty said. He liked hospitals and X-Rays.

"Hmmm," the doc said. "I don't know about that."

Then the doc started to explain to the parents—talking right over Marty's head to them—that their son's vision was just plain awful vision, and it would only get worse. "It's not horrible, though," he said. "He may not be the architect on the site, because of the eyes, but he could be laying brick."

Marty's father laughed, shook his head, and whisked Marty and his mother away.

It took months—that doctor with the architect line hadn't diagnosed it right. The doctor with the toxic fluid didn't either. Nor did the MRI dudes. Nor the globe and dot brigade. The man who diagnosed him right had to perform this:

A test: Tilt your head back so I can drip this topical anesthetic in your eyes. Drop. Drop. Now place your head in this metal holster, resting your chin here. I'm going to clip your eyelids with a little pincher to hold them open, OK? Now, I'm going to adhere clear electrodes onto your eyeballs, like contacts with wires sprouting out. Keep your eyes straight ahead: watch this TV screen that will be showing snow, for, I don't know, an hour? Do nothing else. The nurse will moisten your eyes.

Then, days later, in a regular doctor's office—POP—"You have Stargardt's disease!"

"Star Gazer," Marty said.

"It's a one in 10,000 shot. Macular degeneration. Your Parvomagnular cells in your fovea have died and because of—"

This was lost on him.

The analogy that Marty gives people today goes like this: think of seeing, of vision, of taking in visual stimuli as being in a movie theater. You have the world and its light, which are the images from the projector. You have the lens over the projector that focuses the light onto a screen, which acts just like the lens on your eye, focusing the light and images from the world onto your retina. Your retina is the screen. In the center of the retina is the macula. Now, go to a movie theater, and, before the film starts, rip apart the center of the screen. You have Stargardt's disease.

All Marty's got is peripheral vision. When he looks right at something, it vanishes. The cells in the center of his eye are dead. They do not register any stimuli. But when he's looking around, reading a book, or checking out ladies at the beach he doesn't see a nothing in the middle of the everything. His brain has ceased to interpret information from those cells, because they have been crying wolf for so long now. Marty can make his brain listen to (look at) what is in the center, when he wants to. All this does is create a floating blob of nothingness. He does this for fun.

Marty has been told to write about Stargardt's disease. Create a character with it. Give him a dilemma. Make the effects of the disease inform the dilemma in enlightening ways. Have the character physically unable to see what is directly in front of him while at the same time never being emotionally able to feel what is directly in the middle of his emotions. But that's impossible. It's too perfect. The metaphors too easy. The disease so rare that its appearance in a story would be blatantly conceptual. Red-flag-artifice. No one would believe it or care about its many meanings in his life.

A test: Create a character. Give him this weird eye disease, where he can't look right at anything, cannot stare directly, truthfully, at the dilemma. Now give him the dilemma.

WEDNESDAY AFTERNOON

The announcement comes. "The 3:16 PM Providence/Stoughton commuter train, making the following station stops..." I hear where I am to go. Which track. I run.

The ride is always uneventful. But short.

It's a beautiful day. Blue and open. Warm with purpose.

It feels not a lot like work, but all the anxiety that accompanies not seeing the big board makes the commute frustrating, which helps me feel as though mine is a realer life than usual. Feeling an amount of irritation, a touch of dread about whether I'll get wherever on time, this all reads as if I'm contributing or doing what we are supposed to do in this life: amass tiny hardships.

At the Ruggles stop, Northeastern University area, a man enters my car with a tennis bag hanging on his shoulder. He's got the same build as my father, and he's aged appropriately. But he doesn't care that the racquets bang against each of the seats as he walks down the aisle. Doesn't even notice, maybe, when the door to the next car clips the bag. I put this man in the center of my field of vision. I look right at him. And he's gone.

TENNIS

[13? 14? YEARS BEFORE?]

Tennis began as racquetball. His dad had a tournament, and Matt was—he doesn't know—still describing his age with quarters and halves. His dad handed Matt a racquetball racquet to play with before he entered a giant glass box to face an opponent.

In a hall of racquetball courts, sounds come to the ear with the unpredictable variations in loudness and frequency of what it must be like for the heart listening to the pops and blasts from the upstairs brain-room. The tournament was big and scary, and—because his dad was participating in it—important. It was what men did.

After his match—and Matt still doesn't know if they are called matches in racquetball, or if that is reserved for chess and tennis—Dad took him into one of the glass boxes and showed Matt how to swing a racquet. His father dropped the little blue sphere on the hardwood, let it bounce, and then swung slowly, showing, teaching. Matt tried to imitate. His shots dribbled to the far white wall, miss-hits probably all of them. His dad said, "Good." Good. Miss-hit after miss-hit. He showed Matt again and again. He let the ball bounce, swung with the deliberateness of a teacher, instructing. He made it look easy. Matt was just too young.

But that was the beginning of tennis. The first swings with a racquet and a ball. The first time with a racquet in his hands with his father.

Matt never entered another glass box in his life, and neither did his father, as far as he knows. Racquetball's for punks.

WEDNESDAY AFTERNOON

switch of perspective

My mother's black Ford Explorer is just nowhere around when I reach the top of the hill at the Route 128 train station in Canton. She's late. I begin the walk down Green Lodge Street. Only a mile and a half away is her home. It's lovely out. Green and covered. Warm with found time. I swing an invisible racquet. I look over the overpass, down to the Neponset River, where I lost so many lures in my youth.

Here comes Mom's big black truck, racing around a turn on two wheels.

"You were busy?" I falsely accuse through the passenger window.

"Stuff it, Mark."

I'm smiling. There's no way she's had obligations.

The drive is always nice. Green Lodge is a scenic way and boasts about it on its sign. Cruising back to the house, there's a nationally protected forest on the left side and a nine hole private golf course on the right. My folks were invited to join that club when they moved to the street, but they refused for reasons that have yet to satisfy my curiosity. I mean, there's golf and tennis. Here on the street. What gives? I once saw a deer jump over the fence that nationally protects the woods. That fence is eight feet high. Amazing. The green. The moss. The leaves. The bowing oaks and maples and beeches. Animate. Saying welcome back.

We pass the Shaw's house. Katie and I knew each other in kindergarten. No idea where she is now. The MacDuff's place, sitting on the hill of the third tee box, pristine colonial with cool blue pool and excellent clam bakes. The Forsythe's red house on a slope. Mrs. Forsythe worked for the admissions at a private high school that I applied to and to which I did not receive admittance. A grudge? The Franklin's white mansion set way off the road, barely visible through the trees. A giant. A scary place, where I used to play football in the side yard. Benny is now a famous Latin scholar. His father served time in prison, published his diary of the incarceration in the *Boston Globe*. A weird read. He also ran for mayor. The Clarks, with whom all of us were/are-ish the closest. Jeff with his four-fingered hand, pointer finger lopped off in a shop accident before we met him. The boys, Christopher and Peter with their wives and condos and financial jobs now. Melanie, the youngest, her parents died in a plane crash when she was five, and her mother's sister, our neighbor, Jennifer, took her in. Melanie calls Jeff and Jennifer Dad and Mom. She's in college. At the end of the street, past where we will be turning for our driveway is another family's house with a small farm. Horses and such. I used to feed them carrots with my dad.

And we're home.

"Carl came by and organized your room and took out the recycling last night. He's so funny," says my mom while entering the house and indicating the freshly cleared-out section of the garage where two weeks' worth of milk cartons, take-out boxes, diet ginger ale bottles, and coke cans had previously accrued.

Carl is my oldest friend. He lives a mile away, at his mother's place. Heart-of-gold type kid. Largely underemployed. Too-smart-for-society type. He sleeps little. I imagine him sometimes in his mother's house. At 4 AM. Organizing and reorganizing his mother's things. His clothes into piles. Listening to talk radio. Taking apart computers. Placing circuits in new locations. Washing one shirt. Drying one sweater. Never sleeping. My heart breaks for this. He could do anything, but he's held up by his issues, too. I wish we could combine forces, help each other in a beautiful friend way to figure everything out and carry each other into grand and green futures.

"Oh, he also organized and went through all your old papers, stories and writings from school."

"What the fuck did that asshole do!?"

FRENZIED/SCATTERED STORY BY A MESSED UP KID, NEVER SHOWN TO ANYONE

[FOUR YEARS AFTER]

"Arrhythmia, Arrhythmia"

When I was six months old we moved out of a house that had a tiny creek running through its backyard. "You came and we knew we needed a bigger house," Mom always said. No, she said it like twice and I remembered it over and over. And I believed her. She should've known that about me. It was dangerous.

I wanted to be my dad. A posterboard drawing with red and green crayon spelled out: "I want to be an anesthesiologist." My dad was something to brag about until he had an arrhythmia while playing tennis at the Blue Hill country club with three other doctors. Arrhythmia. Arrhythmia. It's the name of a flower that blooms whenever it wants to. "Another patient died on the table." These were our dinner conversations sometimes. He ate Ring Dings after most meals. And he was my hero.

A friend got me into Led Zeppelin late in life, sort of. Listening to "Over the Hills and Far Away" in the dark, smoking a cigarette and dreaming viciously of romantic silences with a blonde girl at college—I just can't wait to get up tomorrow and see what she says to me. I plastered my room with pieces of paper that had the same line on it over and over. The line was: "Insert inspiration [here]." I wasn't doing well, but I wasn't doing as bad as that. I was doing pretty adolescent.

I tower in front of Dad's grave—well, I'm on my way there. I have to drive by his site to get to Movie Madness. There are other rental places, but this one has an adult section. Through the half-opened passenger window I look over to the cemetery and think that I will stop now, but then I can always stop on the way back. Then again I don't want to stop at his grave with all this porno in sight. He can't see anymore and I really don't believe he's anywhere near me. I just go home. It's not exactly *life in the face of death*.

Mom brought a little basket of flowers and twigs and leaves and things from the yard. It was his birthday or whatever it was then—an anniversary. A reason to go. An obligation. She put two little decorative presents in the basket—the kind you would pin on top of a real present. Cute. "Mom! Get those the Hell out of there. Do it! Now!" Hard cry, grunts. Mom sorry, scared. Never again.

"Manny, I just heard. I was away and I just heard…"
[The faint sound of guitar chords on an unamplified electric guitar.]
"Thanks, man."
"You sound OK. Man, I don't know how I'd be if my dad died."
"You know me."

Trying to feel normal with a friend at the mall, in a sporting goods store, I saw a tennis racquet. I walked out of the store, sat down on a bench in front of Fanny Farmer and wailed so that people in the L-shaped alcoves of the mall wondered where the sirens were coming from.

After his death, I noticed our major differences. I realized that I hated "Seinfeld." In the hospital waiting room Jerry told George and Elaine that his girlfriend had man hands. All along I thought that Dad and I shared the laughter. But, no, I hated "Seinfeld" just as much as my brother hates San Francisco. When Mom called, he walked down the streets, missing speeding cars—missing death by inches. Right then he realized that he was more wild than his father. He paid over a thousand bucks to fly home from San Francisco and has never returned. He realized as soon as Dad died how he actually didn't love the hilly city that our father had adored. So, we waited until he died to hate things that he liked. Luckily, or else the house would have been turned upside down.

"I'm no role model," says my friend who's imitating an ad.

"Actually, Lester, who is your role model?" I think it's the first serious thing I've ever asked him.

"Jordan. Can you dunk?"

And that is good enough for me. I can't dunk, but I think that if I could I would go to a gym every single day and do it. I would jump from the foul line and glide, whimsically kicking my feet all the way to the hoop. I would turn 360 degrees in the air and hang from the rim. I would lob the ball high and go up and fetch it, throw it down with an emphatic flush, and yell. I would jump up and slam. Slam. Slam. I would fly. I would soar up to a hundred foot hoop and dunk the ball, then climb up on top of a crystal backboard and scream at the clouds. Then the next day I would do it again. Without money—without food—I would finally be free and eager.

Two years after my father's heart went bump ba ba bump, instead of bump ba bump, screeching tires and singing woke me from a dream in which a word on a piece of notebook paper erased itself more and more as I leaned in to read it again and again. I clicked on the lamp that my brother built for me in woodshop (the switch is a pump for a water spigot) and looked at my window. On my lawn, a bonfire and a group of barefoot men and women held hands and circled the flames, chanting in a language I couldn't decipher. But I realized that the truly remarkable phenomenon was in the middle of my two panes of glass. A condensation portrait of my father's face had spread into existence. His broken nose, his freckle under his left eye, his receding hairline—all of his face, his disembodied head hovered in my window frame. A misty, gray water painting.

After that, newscasters showed up, police cruisers bookended our street, local celebrities sang for the masses on our driveway, people wearing purple T-shirts that read "We Believe!" bought Coca-Colas from a hot dog vendor in a white chef's hat near my old swing set. Football teams in gold helmets and green uniforms came and got down on one knee on our sidewalk before their Sunday afternoon gridiron match-ups. The news broadcasts referred to me as "The Chosen One." Then one night, I broke the window and sent all the tourists away. Some said in the newspapers that I had shattered the only proof of God. Some said that I should be persecuted. I said I was going through a hard enough time without all these people and their offerings every day. I wanted to be alone—so I went to college where no one knew me or my dad and I could get drunk and break shit and be anonymous. No one asked. One girl asked and I told her, but I knew that when I was telling her that I was only telling her because I listened to Led Zeppelin late at night and thought of her and that maybe she would give me a pity kiss.

I was looking for extraterrestrial support at my dad's gravesite. I sat there for ten hours. I had to hop the fence because they close cemeteries at night. I wanted to give up on trying to figure out all this bizarre stuff on my own and really get some weird otherworldly advice. I thought that if I sat there long enough, something would happen. Maybe a Hamlet scene without the vengeance—maybe a ghost that would whisper: "Plastics." I wanted it so bad. So bad. I wanted something else to tell me what was what. I wanted to know how you know when a girl likes you. I wanted to know how you can stay happy and make money, how to throw a curve, how to sail far away. I wanted some ghost of the cemetery to tell me that life was really something other than life—that I was already dead and so that I could do whatever I wanted because it turned out that everything worked in reverse from what we thought on earth. That you have to die to be alive. I wanted someone to tell me that you don't need to understand everything that leads up to the one thing you want to know. I wanted that ghost to say that my father wasn't a good man after all so I can go out and live without guilt. I wanted Dad to appear to me with a ghostly mistress and say that he was having a grand old time and that I could go and live an anxiety-free existence, looking forward to death. Maybe the moon would be out the night that I am thinking of and it would be full and I would finally be of the age to grow into the werewolf I had always been but didn't know because I hadn't matured. I lay on my stomach by his grave, hoping to God that something would take over for me, something other than me would guide me—that I could find a role model in the dirt.

When I turn my brain on and it is really going to town on all my thoughts, all I can do is sit down and smoke a cigarette and yell at my girlfriend in the middle of one of her sentences involving the word "Hard." That's when I'm not listening anymore—when I stand up again and start yelling real loud at her and saying things that don't make much sense to her. When I scream out the words "How can you! Do you ever think of me? I walk around every day with this!" That's when I'm sublime—it is what I seek. What I seek is that zombie inside of me that reaches out and hurts those who love me—that's when I can taste pain. When I hang up the phone I can smell the fury, I can touch the air and see its temperature. I can breathe out and feel exorcised.

Paris, 2002. Nighttime. The bar around the corner from apartment in the 18th, La Chope du Chateau Rouge. It's run by welcoming and cool Algerians. One of them, Marzuka, comes reeling up to me and says: "The Best of the Best."

I say, "Tu as eu beacoup des biers, mon ami." I can speak French better when I'm drunk. Or I'm drunk enough to think so.

Marzuka tells me that that is his favorite movie.

"That movie sucks, Marzuka," I say in English.

"Marzuka says, "Comment?"

"Votre film, Marzuka, est merde." Marzuka doesn't strike me as smart, but it's hard to tell with the language barrier. Marzuka goes and gets my drink and tells the people around me to get the hell out because he has something to say to me.

"Manny, American!" Marzuka looks at me. I think of home, hearing *American*. I suddenly realize the date. I am across the Atlantic on the anniversary of my father's death. I have run so far, so fast, I have held my breath so long that I got away. These French people look like angels to me, speaking their language that sounds like the names of a million exotic plants. This one lady has on a sequin and see-through top. Her breasts are white as the moon.

"Je suis desole. Aujourd'hui est l'anniversaire de le mourt de mon pere."

"Oh, mon vieux."

"Merci."

While Marzuka tells me something nervously, practicing his English, I think about my mother at home with her blanket around her feet, watching "Law and Order", and thinking of my father because it is the thing to do. I hope she is not thinking of me, though. I don't want her to see me like this.

The next beer and the next beer and next, they push reality back a foot, then two, then three. It's safer now. I interrupt Marzuka, who is practicing English-as-a-Third-Language by telling me the plot of movies we both know. I use rapid English, quicker than I know he'll be comfortable with. I get it out fast. I tell Marzuka all about how my father died and what I did in the following weeks. "He went off to play tennis, and my girlfriend came over, and we ate pizza and watched a movie, and in the evening, the phone rang, and I answered and Dr. Hutch said, 'Mark, I need to talk with your mom,' then, just madness, my mother and I hugged each other fiercely, we held tight, and we were frantic, and out of all the scary crazy thoughts, what kept coming out of my mouth was a broken shriek, over and over again, just, 'What!? What!? What!?'"

Marzuka continually tells me that he can't understand, slow down. But I grab his monstrous hand and keep him there, look at his face, his confusion, and go on and on. "And the nurse told me that I could go look at him, but I chose not to, and my mother did and I never have the option now, ever again, is that wrong?—that I didn't want to see him dead, my mom said that if I wanted to, he was still warm."

Marzuka struggles from my grasp and brings me a beer, shaking his head.

"It's today!" I shout at him. "Today is the day he died, and here I am, drunk, so far away!" Is this any way to honor the anniversary of his death? "Marzuka, listen to me: my dad died, and I am here. I miss him. I don't know what to do. What do you say?"

Marzuka pats me on the shoulder. He shrugs. He clinks my beer bottle.

After the bar closes up, I walk down through the night to the river. I had put the words out, said it out loud. I heard myself say it all out loud. Marzuka heard, if not understood.

When the sun comes up over the Seine, I open my eyes, there on a city bench, to an easier morning.

But slowly, more and more, nothing hurts. I forget what the embarrassment felt like when the show "Father Knows Best" was referenced on TV in mixed company. When someone tells a story of their father, they don't hesitate anymore in front of me. Bit by bit I am no longer grieving. Piece by piece people aren't careful with me. And when I play tennis these days, I think about my dad's serve—I use his racquet and I laugh so hard when I miss-hit one into the fence. I wonder sometimes if Tom or my girlfriend or Lester remembers that my dad is dead when they are talking with me. I wonder if they know with every goose pimple on their neck that I am missing something very important right now. I wonder if they can still smell the scent of Arrhythmias blooming in the desert of my heart. But how could they? How could they, when each day, for a little longer and little longer, I keep forgetting that I'll never see him again.

WEDNESDAY EVENING

"Mark, what are you doing? Reading over your old stuff?"

"I need to see something."

"Can you just stop. Put that down. Talk to me, please."

"I just. Did Carl see... Some secret... Fine. Is there coffee?"

"Yes. Don't use that mug. It's chipped. Here."

"Why do you keep broken things?"

"So you'll go to the meeting next Wednesday?"

"What is that? What am I doing there?"

"I told you."

"You were scant on details."

"I told you. Were you listening?"

"You didn't tell me anything."

"I told you: Suzanne's friend has a son in high school who lost his dad, and he isn't doing well. He's just not handling it. Maybe you can talk with him."

"Where? What will this look like? You're still buying this milk?"

"The other milk ran out. I get the organic milk when I go to the supermarket. But last night I just ran out of it. I get the other stuff when I can."

"You are always talking about how you care so much about animals. But you get this stuff."

"Leave me alone. I get the other stuff when I can."

"What is happening?"

"There's a bereavement group that meets every other week, and Suzanne asked me to ask you if you would maybe talk with this kid."

"So, I'll sit there, during the meeting?"

"Yes."

"And what? Take him aside afterward?"

"Just talk with him."

"Give him my business card?"

"Something."

"Do I have to share in this? What is the set up?"

"You'll go along. You don't have to share, if you don't want."

"You're going?"

"Say hi to Lady."

"My back hurts. I can't reach down."

"She's your dog, too. She wants you to say hi."

"Hi, Lady."

"Pet her, Mark."

"How did he die?'

"Who?"

"The kid's dad."

"I don't know."

"So, I'm supposed to be—"

"He just needs to see that you've been through this, and after time, you arrive somewhere."

"So, I'm like the healed one?"

"You are at a point much later than him, and he needs to see someone young, who lost his father and is now better."

"Better?"

"Been through a lot."

"Ten years, Ma."

"I know. I know. It seems like yesterday, doesn't it, Mark?"

"In ways."

"It sometimes feels like forever ago. And it sometimes feels like yesterday."

  My mom sighs.

"I'll do it. I'll go with you."

"Ten years?"

"Ten years after."

DENZEL WASHINGTON MOVIE

[DAYS AFTER]

It's a gruesome act of awareness to try to enjoy a common thing so soon after a tragedy, but you have to fill the days. You have got to stuff the senses with stuff to sense, so you and your mom and your bro found yourselves renting movies and watching them. Millions of them. VHS tapes. Bags of them at the chain video rental store. So, you were watching a movie with Denzel Washington in it.

There you were: on the couch, in a line. Mom on the right, you in the middle, your brother on the left. You were staring at this crime movie, trying to follow the plot instead of your wild thoughts, when Denzel says, "one important event divides life into before and after."

Your mom says, "That's for sure." She tells you and your bro that you know that for sure.

If it's so for sure, does it matter where it comes from? Does it matter that this truism came from a movie you can't even remember the title of now? You don't think so anymore. There's a person behind every word. No matter where from. Animals and trees can't speak. Yet. Everyone is a writer, even if they only talk. Say things.

WRITING WORKSHOP

[TWO YEARS AFTER]

It was a nonfiction writing workshop—Personal Essay—but Mitch was writing fiction. Not even realist fiction. No one noticed or spoke up if they had suspicions. He knew the professor knew, and she chose to let him go with it. Mitch wrote a story about a woman morphing into a monster, for crying out loud, for laughing in quiet!—didn't even mask the illegal enterprise. That story dealt with the monstrosity he saw in people who looked disturbed by passing ambulances, blaring sirens. But it was fiction, and she knew it, and he just kept writing the fake stuff, never saying his own personal things he had to personally say.

The nonfiction professor emailed Mitch one night.

She told him her aunt was dying and her cat was dying. The email had a drunken-consciousness. This, the first email ever received from this professor, and there Mitch sat, reading about her aunt and her cat, the two buying their tickets to the boneyard. Death. Grief. Something he was into. He pictured his young professor, swaying about in her apartment, swilling wine, sidling up to the computer desk with slippery eyes, opening up her email account and typing in his address. It was late at night when she did this. Red wine in a yellow mug. This was her first semester at the college, Mitch's third. She must have been renting an apartment, the kind they had so many of in that town—apartments constructed within old Victorian mansions. Nooks. Crannies. A general warpedness. Looking down her short hallway, from the entrance to the closet, the door on the right not quite fitting its frame anymore, a claw foot tub whose charm had gone missing, a lukewarm bath foregone this particular night for hot wine. There must have been a slant to that hallway, the wood floor sloping almost imperceptibly from east to west, making each step, every day, every swaying drunken lonely night, a cause to consider her own stability both physically and emotionally. Steps in bare feet down this hallway with the too close wallpapered walls, the too high ceiling that sometimes grew while she slept, the light with its metal string hanging down to be pulled but never being pulled because the light was bad and becoming just another listing figure in there, rising out of reach. She drank and stepped around in there. She stepped all around in this place. One night, slipping in the warpedness, her fingers landed on the keyboard and transmitted a warbling message to Mitch.

He wrote a response but deleted it.

For the rest of the course, Mitch attended class. Handed in his fictions. Received his comments and grades. Met in her office for one-on-one feedback sessions.

Mitch began to notice her clothes. Knee-length skirts of solid color—emerald, ruby. Her hair was never windblown. Opaque tights. He can't remember her shoes.

She did not return to teach the following year. Mitch still hasn't written an honest personal essay, a full true piece of nonfiction.

WEDNESDAY EVENING

I have earned impunity for the day by agreeing to go to this thing, this group meeting that my mother must understand is something I will not do easily. So, I can go back to reading through my old stories and fake personal essays and plays and half screenplays and crummy poetry from college and graduate school and high school and private times on vacations to search for something true and honest and personal that I wouldn't want Carl to read. But I don't. I drink coffee and stare at the broken cupboard under the stove in the kitchen. You can see a jagged crack running right from the top of the cupboard to it's base, two inches from the hinges on the left, so that if the cupboard were not *clearly* super-glued back together, part of the cupboard would be there, only about two inches of it with the hinges, exposing all the cluttered pots and pans within. I stare at the stove above this brokenness, an electric range that my mom's always wanted to upgrade. Two of the four burners are on permanent leave from duty. Like us. The windows over the sink haven't had screens in years. The bay window by the kitchen table is two-paned, and within the panes, moisture has entered, remaining therein. There is a misty blotch obscuring the view of the backyard. All the plants in front of that window are fakes, frauds. The ceiling's got heavy water damage, drawing wild orange and brown oblongs up there. A week's worth of newspapers, still wrapped in their cellophane, sit on the chairs. One has been kicked into a corner below the table. A jacket, the owner of which might be dead, hangs eternally on the back of the door. I once threw out a can of soup in my mother's kitchen that was dated ten years ago. I just stare. Admire.

MOUNTAIN DEW

[EVOLVING BEFORE]

Ours was the house of soda and candy. Ours was the house of air hockey tables, Ping-Pong tables, indoor Nerf hoops. Ours was the house of spare rooms above the garage refinished to accommodate friends and sleepovers, to keep the noise away from the sleeping parents. Ours was the house of roof access. Ours was the house of midnight skinny-dipping. Ours was the house of cigarettes and marijuana out the window through a fan, surreptitious beers and liquor in through the window. Ours was the house of pissing out the windows. The house of Sega, Genesis, 32X, Turbo Graphix 16, Sega CD, PlayStation, PlayStation 2. Ours was the house of illegal cable and late night free porn. The house where first kisses happened, where first breasts, first dicks and pussies got seen and enjoyed. Ours was the house off the road. Ours was the house of an endless supply of alcoholic liquids in the basement, stored up from our dad's Navy days—liquids from every corner of the globe. Ours was the house with sometimes-nitrogen tanks and lab coats. Ours, the house of five CD changers and speakers the size of refrigerators. The house the pizza delivery guy got a huge tip from because the credit card was available for any food purchases. Ours was the house of indestructible coffee tables: burnt, stained, upended. The house of convenient flat hand mirrors and prescription bottles that were finally liberated from backpacks, spread out over desks, and allowed to roll. The house that lured first the soda-seeking elementary schoolers, then the videogame crazed, then the daring curious first-time drug users, then the longtime drug users, then the video game crazed and soda-seeking drinkers and druggers. Ours was the house of all this for a while. Ours was the house of Mountain Dew, which our father drank morning, noon, and night. Mountain Dew, a radioactive-colored sugar and caffeine concoction. A bite in the jowls. A tingling in the esophagus. A cool plunge into the stomach. A pinch in the head. An awakening. Energy. Drink. The smell of lemon/lime pine needles. Pins and needles in the nose. Fucking Hyper Green Taste! Ours was the house of showerheads that rained green. Ours, the house whose faucets dripped green. The house whose patriarch's heart pumped green. We wish you could've seen it!

NAPKINS

[MONTHS AFTER]

Douglas walked in through the mudroom door from a day's work. Now it was nighttime. Mason was in his room, finishing up homework. Mom was in the kitchen, whisking eggs and milk into a bowl next to a plate of breadcrumbs, the chicken fillets already rinsed and ready and the burners already warming. Douglas kissed Mom on the cheek, removed his winter coat, and headed up to say hey to Mason and ask how school went today.

The two brothers shared a laugh when Mason told Douglas about how a friend of his at school had made an announcement at assembly about a stolen case of CDs. This friend had implored the school's community to 'sack up' and return the CDs. "He actually said 'sack' in front of the whole school!" Good laugh, then Douglas was in the kitchen with shirt sleeves rolled up, asking his mother if he could help with anything.

"No no. I've got it. You just relax. You worked all day."

OK, thought Douglas. He grabbed a can of Mountain Dew from the refrigerator, went to the living room, and put on the Celtics pregame show.

Douglas could hear his mother put on music from the other room. She put on a James Taylor album. It played through the computer speakers in the kitchen. This was the first time in a long time that his mother had put on music. It was significant. He looked at his Mountain Dew, looked at the Celtics starting lineups, listened to the music from the Kitchen, music he remembered from times past, from his childhood, from riding around in his mother's car, listening to her sing along to that music. This was music from riding around in his dad's car, his mother putting in the CD. He remembered driving along a beach somewhere—all of them, including Mason—as a neat and clean family, somewhere fun and honest. Douglas smiled on the couch.

Soon enough, Mason joined him with his own can of Mountain Dew. The two commented on the basketball season thus far, their complaints so far. It turned out that the team was having a bad year, but maybe, if this new talent, Paul Pierce, could figure out how to play an all-around game, the team would have a shot next year. Things were getting better. The team would return to glory, they thought. They were hopeful for this return.

Mom called the boys to the kitchen table, where she had set up three placemats, three plates, three knives, and three forks. She placed the serving plate of chicken fillets on a mat in the center of the table. She placed the rice and carrots in bowls on either side. Steam rose from the table, smells wafted up, smells that conjured: this was a classic meal of Douglas's mother's. This meal, with its sights and smells, was a staple of the family's week. The kind of thing that can bring you back, return you to other times.

Douglas sat at the head, Mason took his usual seat, and Mom was still flitting around asking who wants what to drink? But Mason and Douglas coaxed her to the table: Mom, come, sit, eat, we're fine, we are all fine, now join us. She did.

The boys waited for their mother before they began forking themselves chicken and spooning out rice and carrots.

There was another fixture on the table, though. A basket made of paper-thin, woven slats of wood. It was such a constant at the table that one wouldn't notice after a time. There was never a need for this basket to be picked up, never a need for this little basket to be anywhere but on the table, day in, day out, season in, season out. For years it sat in its same spot. Maybe for all time.

The sole function of this little basket was to hold light blue paper napkins. And it had done so forever. Douglas couldn't remember ever filling the basket with napkins. In fact, he had never even thought about it, so he wouldn't be forced to try to recall this. Mason was never one to help out with chores. The little basket stood there for as long as any of them could remember, filled with napkins. A never-ending supply of light fluffy disposable napkins. The little basket must've regenerated them, at night. No one ever questioned it. It was just there for all time with napkins in it. The three didn't even notice it anymore.

"Tell Mom the story you told me about Hedly at school today, Mason," said Douglas, forking his first piece of chicken and anticipating a wonderful dinner.

And Mason did begin his story for his mother. Mom knew Hedly, and she was going to crack up at this story. The boys knew it. It was the best part of their day to know that one of them had a story that was going to cause their mother to crack up and laugh her laugh.

Douglas kept his eyes on his mom, waiting for the moment wherein the story Mason would shout 'sack up,' which is crude and tasteless but just the sort of thing that his mom couldn't help but crack up at while declaring through her laughter, 'oh, that's awful.' Douglas watched her with a smile while his hand floated over to the little basket. This motion, this moving of his hand to the basket was almost an involuntary action controlled by the nervous system within him. So common to the atmosphere, with the music and the can of Dew, and Mason telling a story, and his mother about to laugh, and the smell of chicken filets, rice and carrots, the low-hanging light directly over the center of the table, casting a light that was such a regular light to him, for all of this was such routine, so familiar and normal. His hand floated over the basket and ducked in to extract a napkin. His hand hit the bottom of the basket. His fingertips touched the woven wooden slats on the bottom of the basket for the first time. His hand jumped straight out of the basket. Douglas turned worried eyes to the basket, flipped it on its side to look inside.

Mom took her eyes off Mason, focused them on Douglas' hand. Douglas reached with his other hand to the basket, picked the thing up, and searched inside. They all looked inside, and they all saw that the basket was empty.

Everything stopped. The story. The music. The anticipation of a laugh. The light being normal and good. The steam stopped rising from the table. It all ended.

Douglas got up from the table.

"What are you doing?" asked Mom.

"Doug?" said Mason.

Douglas exited the kitchen and returned with his winter coat.

"Douglas?" said his mother.

"Doug," said Mason.

Douglas walked through the mudroom door to the garage. Mason and Mom heard the car start. They just watched the door in silence.

Douglas' car could be heard returning, five minutes later. Mason and Mom remained at the table. Douglas entered in through the mudroom door, carrying under his arm three bags full of light blue napkins. He went to the table, ripped open a package of napkins, stuffed them in the little woven basket, removed his coat, and put it on the back of his chair. Douglas picked up his fork, cut a small piece of chicken, and ate it. He floated his hand over to the basket and grabbed a napkin without looking. He wiped his mouth and placed the napkin on his lap.

"Where were we?" Douglas asked and smiled.

Mason slowly began his story again. The music started up softly and cautiously from behind the counter. The light tiptoed back up to its familiar glow over the yellow table. The steam began to rise meekly again from the table.

Everything wanted to return to normal.

WEDNESDAY EVENING

I don't want to train it back into Boston, but I do want to leave, now that the house has presented its newness, its flaws, and my mother is watching daytime television with the little dachshund curled up next to her.

I call Carl.

"Yaar?" says Carl. It's past six at night and this is obviously the first human interaction he's had. Possibly in days. Most likely he's been sleeping since the sun rose.

"Did I wake you, friend?"

"No. Nah!" A clear fumbling to get out of bed accompanies his shouts. Carl has a unique undiagnosed disorder that I've never seen in anyone else, and I was a psych major: Carl will never admit to having been woken up by your call, by your knock on the door, by your shaking him awake. He will claim to have been up. Someone once attributed this to Carl's politeness. It is not a pride issue, not that he won't admit to having the very human need to sleep, but it is because he doesn't want you, the rouser, to feel as though you've bothered him in any way. I say, even when he is asleep on your couch and you are slapping him due to his religious snoring. A snore like a god's.

"Since you're up, you want to head into town with me? I'm at Green Lodge."

"Sure. Let me—"

"Thanks."

Carl's car is a 1990 white Honda Civic. He owned one once before, and his mother purchased him a Volkswagen. He drove the German beast for a year or so, then sought out and purchased the same 1990 white Honda Civic he previously owned. The Volkswagen sits in the driveway of the house his mother now resides in.

I put on my seatbelt as we enter I-93 N toward the Bean.

"Don't trust me?"

"Ha," I say. "I see you organized my stories."

"Yeah," he says while turning on talk radio and sneezing. I turn the radio off.

"Consult me before doing that again."

The windows get rolled down. Cigarettes get lit. The radio battle wages on.

"I'm going to a bereavement group meeting next week."

"What?"

"Not for me. Not for my bereavement."

"Oh."

"My mom was asked by a friend of friend or something. There's a kid whose father died. He's in high school. I'm supposed to heal him."

"Whoa."

"Yeah. I guess I'll talk to him."

"Huh."

We stop off for beers that Carl buys. More cigarettes. A Celtics Preseason game is on tonight, and we've gone too long without basketball. We are going to get drunk and watch. I don't toss Carl any cash.

Carl hasn't seen his father in I don't know how long. The last I heard of him, Carl told me that his father was drunk at his cabin in Vermont. Drunk and firing a pistol at the ceiling of his new cabin, trying to shoot a bat. What an image! When he told me, we both laughed. I ask him to tell me that story again now. This time I want to see if I can discern Carl's feelings on the subject. I want to know if he wants something different. See if fathers are just fathers. You want them.

"He just shot the gun, trying to kill a bat. I don't know."

I hold in the laugh.

Carl laughs. He laughs in the way that he's expecting my harmony. I hold it in.

GAREWOOD, POTENTIAL FATHER

[FIVE YEARS AFTER]

Garewood was the professor Michael had returned to his old college town to visit. Michael had sent him a story (he can't remember which now), and Garewood agreed to meet and discuss the piece. This favor was significant. After graduating, he had thought his access to the great writer would vanish. He thought his own writing wouldn't be good or serious enough to interest the man. Michael felt unworthy. But then! Miracle of miracles, Garewood kept up correspondence, took Michael's writing seriously, took Michael under a warm wing! But more than that—they had become *close*.

Garewood wasn't available until three in the afternoon, though, so Michael was walking around campus with Professor K., a novelist, an eccentric, a glorious nutcase, who consumed him each time with her honesty, hilarity, and mannerisms. She would, to emphasize a statement, look all around, meeting no one's eyes while tying an invisible string with her fingers, and end her synch and sentence in unison. Tight. Now. Point. Michael thinks he had a crush on her, or he wanted her to have a crush on him that he could reject. But that only happened with uncrushable professors.

Michael asked her what time it was.

"Fuck." He was late. Bad, not traffic late.

"He doesn't mind," she told him. He doesn't know why she figured this.

Michael got on the cell phone and dialed the coffee shop where they were to meet up. "I'm sorry," he told the coffee shop worker.

"This may sound odd, but do you see a slender man about six three, glasses, white push-broom mustache?"

The person did not see this character in the shop.

"Fuck."

Michael arrived on Garewood's doorstep close to an hour after the time he had promised to meet up. The professor opened the door but left the screen closed between the two of them.

"I'm sorry."

"It's OK. I'm upset."

"I'm sorry."

His hand went up. "I'm upset." He closed the door.

The drive from Michael's college town to his apartment in Cambridge is over three and a half hours. Still is. The whole way back, he thought, *I blew it. I just went and ruined something. I worried him, stressed him out, made him think I was dead, vanishing without any word like that, and then revealed myself to simply be a fool. It wasn't a simple inconveniencing. It was deeper. You can't worry caring people like that. What have I just done?*

Days later, with a yellow legal pad and a pen, drafting a letter to Garewood that was supposed to be an apology, Michael saw that his hand had written this line: "though you and I will not have a catch in the backyard, or go fishing together, or share a cigar when my child is born, you are a father to me." When he wrote these words, he knew they were true. He knew it was important and scary because his heart rate increased. They freaked him out. The words were powerful, meaning they could have an effect on Garewood. This string of letters and spaces with the words "father" and the "you" and "me" could cause something to stir, because they were bigger. But big in a private way. This has to do with you, Michael was saying. This *me* has to do with *you*. You have so much to do with who I am. It's the sort of thing that creates more distance. Makes people run.

Who wants sad honesty? Who wants to be a part of someone else's weird life?

Michael thought about everything Garewood had done for him: their first chance encounter in the library of the college. Michael was trying to locate a surrealist novella by Carols Fuentes but couldn't remember the title. He asked Garewood—who happened to be walking through the library, a professor he knew of—did he know this novella? Garewood perked up, thought about it, and the two went off into the stacks to find it together. What a delightful response! A great writer who was just happy to pause and help an interested student. *Aura*, it turned out to be. Michael recalled their first one-on-one meeting, his senior year, trying to discover what should be Michael's project for the advanced fiction class. Garewood read a huge sampling of material, taking so much of his time to sit and read this student's work, just to help. And he encouraged Michael to pursue the strangest and most energetic of the stories, which solidified Michael's belief in the absurd and surreal and wild. Michael recalled Garewood sending off his novella, once completed, to a top tier literary magazine, trying to propel his student's career, demonstrating intimate care and exuberant encouragement. Michael remembered Garewood signing his own books with tender inscriptions; inviting him to play Ping-Pong and actually beating him; suggesting that Michael stay at his house if he needed a place when visiting his old college town; welcoming any stories-in-progress for critique; being a champion of his work; giving untold advice on publishing and conducting oneself; buying the both of them egg salad sandwiches and munching away on his front porch, talking books, talking life choices; Michael remembered everything that was this type of rare and beautiful and formative.

Michael dropped the letter in the mail.

Days went by. Things went by. Stuff.

Michael's been carrying around this belief that everyone can see it on him: this sad fatherlessness. A sad weirdness that warns everyone to be careful with him. Just look at his stories! Death done fabulist, fantastical, absurdist. But that's irrational. That's an irrational thing to believe. Of course, Michael has to play by the same rules as everyone else does. Of course, he should grow up and be honest if he wants someone to talk with him seriously, to know how he feels. He needs to say it truthfully to get what he is after. Michael knew he had fucked up with Garewood.

Then, magically, their relationship was restored. Emails returned to their usual frequency and cheer. Visits were agreed upon. Stories were critiqued.

But it was just this sort of thing that made it impossible. Made Michael realize his real father was gone for good. Gone for bad. Gone for normal. Gone for bizarre. Gone.

Always an awkward silence within a sincere moment between him and an older, dear man. A space. Then an abrupt return of normal things. A moment right before. Then a handshake instead of a hug.

GENIUS

[DEVELOPING WITHOUT]

We like geniuses in fiction. We like to think that it's all chance. We read a book, and declare: GENIUS! We think, lucky them. But also, lucky us for being at least smart enough to recognize genius. Dummies don't see this stuff right. We picture the eccentricity of the genius. We know that it's divine intervention on the page. This makes us happy. We can go on, because we're mediocre. Because it was all chance, and we were not selected. Phew. We can go about our business. Leave it to the madmen, the brilliants. Then we meet a genius, get to be in the same room, office, lodge, hallway, courtyard, bar, Ping-Pong basement with a genius. We get confused. The genius is a nice guy. Smart, sure. But, hey, you know, we can hang with this genius. What the hell? The genius is really generous and supportive and nothing like the odd picture of depraved lunacy we associated with genius fiction writers. We learn of their writing habits. Rigid, but not divine. We piece together that the genius has been writing forever, all the time. Not godstruck with inspiration, but just real practice and dedication. Some talent, sure. But that wasn't exactly what moved the pen over the pages every day for a lifetime. We get nervous that the *onus* is *on us*. We are delighted when we are called protégés. We are tickled that geniuses like our stuff. Are we on our way? We get scared when we meet geniuses who have been so regular that they've been drinkers, druggers, cheaters, when they just love pizza, have 401Ks, post goofy photos on the Internet, when they do the things we thought were reserved for us normals. We hate to learn that they all work way harder than us at this thing of fiction. Wait, it was all supposed to be chance. We get scared that we like our friends too much, like abandoning the practice for parties, for weekends, for television. We like tennis more than sitting alone working on fiction that no one will read. Maybe it is chance. It skipped us, bestowing the talent of dedication on another, whom we call brilliant. We satisfy ourselves. We wait for the date to pass. We call a friend for a three-setter. We run away from the story that needs too much work.

WEDNESDAY EVENING

Nathaniel Hawthorne lived and wrote in and about a small clean attic room. So did Garewood. I try not to kid myself, but my pad's an attic room.

My apartment's right across from a church whose main design feature is the color red. On the day that I moved in, there was a sign out front: "JOIN US FOR THE HIGH HOLY DAYS." Men wearing Yamakas milled about on the sidewalk. It was Passover. This confused me. The following Sunday, hundreds of Koreans poured out of the main door. One day, I saw a woman leave by the side door, and figuring that this was a special door reserved for people in the know, I asked her: "What is this structure's deal?" She informed me that it was indeed a Christian church, but they let out the space for all sorts of things. Jews surrounded by crucified Christs. Sader plates rotting in the back room during sermons. Matzoh for communion. A hymn harmonizing with the Kaddish. She told me I could definitely come by. I am half Jewish (Mom) and half Catholic (Dad). I told her I might just do that.

Tonight, the church fills up my window while Carl and I turn on the Celtics game and crack beer after beer. God is in my window, watching me drink, smoke, write, have sex. With myself. I try not to make much of it. I'd like to believe that I am spiritual. That writing is my spiritual act. But it isn't. It is not spiritual. It isn't even a passion. Writing is hard. It is stressful and rarely transcendent. But the difficulty of it helps me feel that I am alive. The pain that it begets helps me feel that I am part of the human race, because I am not working. I am not having to do the annoying commute. I am allowed to do whatever I want, and what I choose to do is be in pain most of the time, worried about not writing, and stressing out while writing. It is a penance.

The real spiritual part of my life is the Celtics. This year, the team is amazing. Last year, they won the whole thing. I watched the finals on Martha's Vineyard. Alone. Carl watched it at his mother's place. Alone. My brother watched it in LA. Alone. My dad couldn't see them win again, and this is why it is spiritual. He is most with me during the Celtics. Which sounds kind of pathetic. But I am not alone. In this belief.

Carl and I cheer. Carl and I drink. Paul Pierce hits a three. We say: "YAH." Kevin Garnett gets a block, we say: "RAH!" Rondo splits the D, and we say: "OOO AH!" We speak in tongues when the shot clock's low. We meditate during time-outs. We imbibe heavily when the victory is ours. And even more heavily if it is not.

I stand up and replay a crossover and fade away for Carl in my living room, which is really just part of the whole big studio, but I've defined space well in here. Carl mimes a behind-the-back. There is no ball, but we believe in it, even if we can't see it. I rise up, fade away. Look: there's no ball!

RELIGION OVER THE POND

[THREE WEEKS AFTER]

Dream-snap to France and England.

Death can take you places. Like to a crispy yellowed-grass field in the middle of France for your first jump over the pond.

Taize is the name of a town that is the permanent site for a religious camp of sorts. Church services are held three times a day—dawn, after lunch, and ten at night. At each service there is a ten-minute silence. At each service there are thousands of people inside a giant chapel. This is in the middle of France, far from everything we know France for. This field could be in Nebraska. No one I mentioned this town to, while living in Paris, years later, had ever heard of it. I can only assume I actually went there.

You see, for some awesome reason my great friend, Flower, and her family owned a castle in the England countryside, near royalty. Flower was the high school girlfriend of my 'best' friend, Holty. I hung out with him the most, which made him, technically, my best friend. Were we close? We shared things. But I thought I'd do better someday.

The plans were made before my dad blew up—a trip to England and then to Taize with Flower and another friend, Sandy. After he exploded, my mother and brother and Flower and Flower's mom convinced me that it was then even more necessary that I go away and broaden myself. So, less than a month after my father's funeral, I was on a plane over the Atlantic on a holiday that somehow existed outside the new bubble of my dad's death. He wasn't dead yet on that plane. He was alive, respectfully waiting to explode on my return. He would wait for me to have this experience and not ruin it. All the cars in England, driving the wrong way, they were really just rewinding the workings of the earth's clock, and I was not bereft. I remember my time with Flower and Holty like piecing together a dream; it all started when I was my zombie-self and Dad was dead but on hold, too, an undead. I always bounce around all this as if switching scenes while asleep.

Holty didn't want to travel, so I got his spot.

Flower's castle was a castle. It was. It really was. Insane. I couldn't get far enough away to capture the whole thing in the frame of my camera.

We were allowed a night in a hotel—Flower, Sandy, myself—in London. How nuts, right? We went out to a club and drank and danced in a club for the first time in our lives. We were so inexperienced in clubs and ordering alcohol that we ordered a weird bottled drink that we saw on display—V2—and we just kept ordering those, not knowing what they were. They are *filled* with vodka. We got that good drunk you get at the beginning of drinking in life. Flower licked my arm from my fingers up to my shoulder. When I spilled my drink. We all slept in one mess of drunkenness in that crummy hotel in London.

I have a photograph of Flower, Sandy, and myself on Carnaby Street. We are not hung over. That good drinking back then. Cigarettes hidden behind our backs.

You see, Flower's mom is English in a wonderful way. She's got the accent, which is sweet. She's got the castle. She loves her tea. We spent some time together in England, and she was very sweet to me. But no one knows her. I guess I met her.

We hopped on a bus in London after the clubbing night. This bus drove onto a train. The train rode under the English Channel to France and released our bus like a bullet onto the country roads of that country. And after a long time of listening to a Walkman and reading a book probably and hearing that Flower had shaved for sex with Holty we wound up in Taize.

Dream-snap to New England.

Driving away from whatever the heck happened at my dad's funeral, in the limousine, I looked out the window to see Holty stumble on the gradual slope of grass in the cemetery. The tip of his work boot caught on just a piece of nothing in that clean slope of grass and he stumbled a little. Yellow work boots and a suit.

"There's Holty: drunk again," my mom said and giggled. She was referring to Holty's drunken sloppy appearance at my father's wake.

"You know you're my best friend, right?" Holty breathed all over my hands and face that night.

"Yeah," I said and hugged him.

Dream-snap—France.

I was nervous getting off the bus in Taize. It's quite literally a shantytown: forty-foot blue tents in perfect rows make up the living quarters. Square plywood houses for toilets and square molded plastic showers, which I knew immediately I wouldn't be using during this week stay. And an enormous chapel on a hill.

We filled out paperwork—who we were, where we were from, what chores we would be willing to perform. Breakfast, lunch, dinner shifts? Daycare with children? Can you speak French? I wrote that I could speak French and that I wanted to work with children. Really, I just wanted to smoke cigarettes and get drunk again with Flower.

But it worked out. The French thing worked, and I got a pretty easy gig with the kiddies. That was my only real responsibility, it turned out. Everything else was voluntary. Church. Eating. Bathing.

Talking. You could choose a certain vow for the week—silence, fast, vanity. None of us took one, but we all thought they were interesting. We had to talk to one another.

And church.

Jesus!

I had been to church for the first time in years three weeks earlier, carrying my dad's coffin, which was actually rolling on wheels while my bro and I just rested our hands on it. I remember seeing some faces of my friends staring at me as I walked down the aisle. I didn't want them to feel for me. So, I looked forward, touching the casket.

Dream-snap—Canada.

Coincidentally, my first trip over the northern border into Canada was with Flower. I totally forget the circumstances, but we hadn't seen each other in a while. I may have already been out of college at this point. But we drove up there in her Outback, reacquainting ourselves with each other's selves.

We found ourselves in a strip club only after I went into a pharmacy looking for Tylenol #3, which I had heard was illegal in the States and could fuck you up. But it didn't fuck me up at all. What did fuck me up was all the drunk, loose talking Flower and I did. The kind of conversation we had in that strip club, it was as if everything we said could be true and honest. The knowledge came to us like knowledge in a dream, that we wouldn't see each other again for years after this night in a foreign country, albeit Canada. We talked of people who had died. We talked of how odd it was that so many people we know and love don't have beloved dead people in their lives. She admitted to a kind of acute crush on me. Back when we were in England and Taize together. This was shocking. Because I felt the same verboten crush.

"Where are we staying tonight, you think?" I asked her. It was kind of her show at this point.

"We'll just stay at a fancy hotel and put it on my mom's credit card."

"You don't mean that."

"I do. She's with her boyfriend."

"But we have to stay somewhere."

Is this a dream?

"God, I wanted to screw!"

Me? Or the complex closeness the grief of a friend creates? Was this weird niceness coming out wrong? Did the death build a potential for something other than teenaged friendship in the wake of the wake? I felt the strange attraction. Felt it was special, the way she seemed to get how to handle me through my loss. Is death magic?

Snap—France.

The church services were delivered in several languages. Sometimes English. Sometimes French. When I could comprehend, I tried to listen carefully. But I don't remember anything interesting from the sermons. What I do remember are those silences. It's a really simple concept. Silence. There are few things less complicated than sitting as still as possible and not making a noise. But for two thousand people in one room to do this is complicated. First timers, myself notably, look around and wonder what everyone's thinking about. What's on your mind, stranger? Then, you start to think of your own things, or those of us with freshly deceased loved ones, we think of them.

I got back to my blue tent after one of the services to find a folded note on my pillow. It was from Flower's mom.

Dream-snap—A thought.

Sometimes, you see, I think you should envy my death. It's been huge. In this way!

Snap—New England.

Billy Q., in the middle of junior year at that ridiculous private school, he burned his family's multimillion-dollar ocean view house to the ground. It burned down at one of the parties that, inexplicably, I wasn't at.

The week before the house was ash, after a party I was explicably at, Holty met me for our morning-after-a-rager smoke under the back porch.

He told me crudely that he and Flower finally had sex last night.

I didn't respond.

Back in the house, everyone was casually viewing Blazing Saddles on the TV and maybe making breakfast foods. Flower just took a sip of water, sat on the couch, said something to someone that I couldn't hear.

I got a ride home with barely a friend.

Dream-pop—France.

'I like to picture one of the flames on the candles at the front of the chapel as my mother who died several years ago. I know that this is a hard time for you, Mark, and I hope that you can think of your father in a beautiful way here.'

Flower's mom's note was the first note that made me think that other people actually thought of me when I wasn't around. Though I was around, sort of.

One of my tent mates was a guy from Holland named Yoorun.

"He loves you," Flower told me. And Yoorun did love me. He wanted to be around me all the time. He wanted to hear about my life. He wanted to teach me about heavy metal. He always wore this shirt with the band Coal Chamber on it. He was a tough looking dude, but he was here at this religious camp with me and those candles in the chapel and that note tucked in my pillowcase and everything existed outside of time and space. He was, for this paradox, the sweetest person ever.

I'm pretty sure I was cold to him, because all I remember are his words, his offers to go get a beer at the beer tent, his jumping on my back for a piggy ride. His slaps on my back and big huge smiling laughs. His lighting a candle and handing it to me. Jesus Christ I hope that kid's doing well and not angry at people for any of the reasons we can get angry. I hope he's just smiling away and going to heavy metal shows with a heavy metal chick.

And there was another important person there. Flower's best friend from England who was a very pretty girl with a lovely accent, who seemed better than all of us. She was our age, but she had this maturity. More than that. You felt that you were OK, standing next to her. No matter what had happened last night. No matter how you cried in quiet a moment before. You stood next to her, and life was going to go on.

She died in a car crash less than a year later.

Pop—New England.

The other day, on the phone, Holty demanded I call him an asshole. I refused. We were all just messed up teenagers. I should've demanded the same of him and finally been done with all of the guilt. As if it were that simple.

The other day, Flower and her mom were laughing with each other, close daughter and mother.

The other day, I met Flower and Holty's baby girl.

Life!

And all the things in the middle!

THURSDAY MORNING

When I arrive in the morning for the final push to move Anna out completely and over to the new place, I finally get to mention the bereavement group meeting. She is a girl who knows my father through stories. From pictures. Another girl from after. Who doesn't know. Really much. I mention it, not to start a conversation about it, but because bereavement is my thing. I am special in this way. Always for the wrong reasons. This time: as a one-upper to the girl who has nothing whatsoever to worry about. A reminder to her that struggle matters, that she should view me as more lived than she, because of death. She hasn't been through what I've been through. It's my great adventure, and thank God for it, or else I'd be even more undynamic. Thank God for Dad giving me this complication, this instant complexity, or else. If she's seen corners of the world, tasted exotic foods, met indigenous peoples that I've only seen on the Internet, if she's ridden horses or ostriches, jumped out of airplanes and parachuted into canyons, if she's climbed mountains and hang glided back down, she has not experienced my special thing. You can't sign up for it. It's a lottery.

I mention the bereavement to remind her of my uniqueness. I mention it and wait for her response, for her to remember me.

She's putting her unpacked silverware into drawers in her new place. "That's so great. So, you're going to talk with this boy?'

"Yeah." I actually still haven't been able to visualize the event clearly. I have thought that the room will be dark. A woman will speak about her loss. A room full up with all sorts of people will listen. I will spot the kid. He will have hair hanging in front of his face. He will be looking down in a button down shirt, playing with a piece of dirt with his sneaker. He will be obvious. I will spot him, and when the whole thing's done and we are all filling up coffee mugs, I will approach him and say, hello, I'm Mark. That's as far as I've gotten in my imagining of the event. It seems easy if useless.

"You're so good," she says, and this is what I want to hear. I want to hear that I am doing something good, that I am contributing, helping somehow. This pursuit is a noble one and erases my faults, erases my lack of ambition. I am special and can be of special help. She looks at me and she is beaming with pride. Now, it's gone too far. This lie of mine. The lie that I am noble and cool.

"It's no big deal. Probably won't even help the kid."

"You will help. You are so good at this." And I don't know what she's referring to, but maybe she loves me. I play it cool again.

TRUMP CARD

[ONE YEAR AFTER]

Maddox said so many wild and wrong things to girls and girlfriends. So many grandiose statements to potential loves without thinking them through. He's getting better at not doing this so much. He doesn't think he's capable, like before.

Maddox's dad combusted and vanished on a tennis court when he was hanging out with his girlfriend. If you want to psychoanalyze him, this has led to a confusing crossing of wires about the intimacy of girlfriends—they are supposed to become the closest person to you, become a wife with whom you can share anything, share sadness, grief, hard honesty, embarrassing things. But while with a girlfriend, the most massively intimate thing happened, showing him that, actually, girlfriends aren't as important. So, girlfriends posed a particular challenge: Maddox would have to, at some point, fess up to the sadness, the grief. But to do so would make him *different*. If he were to be that close with a girl, it would render the death less intimate. He would replace the significance of the loss with the significance of telling someone else. If he kept the death mysterious, Maddox could ensure that the death was never less important than anything, anyone else.

When Maddox entered college, it was as if the campus were to explode in a week. The feeling of impermanence came from the realization that every single person he was to meet could not have possibly gone through the death with him. No one knew. These people couldn't be close, because he didn't know how to create closeness without simple history doing it for him. These strangers were from the future: the first persons that would be part of Maddox's life as "after-people." All he had were before-people. Now, after people were all around. Looking at him. Not looking at him. Eating. Reading. Falling out of trees. Driving cars. Clapping hands. Being. Is that why he thought the campus would explode soon and all of a sudden?

But there was an advantage to this. Maddox had a great big hard secret that could transform him in the eyes of an after-female from a weird drunk boy into a complicated, deep, and troubled man. Maddox's trump card. If he were face down in puke, knuckles bloodied, and some after-female took care of him for a little, whisking him to a well-lit room with a couch to clean him, Maddox could speak the words. Speak: "my dad vanished right before I got to this after-world." Never a real true private confession. Never intended to reveal any actual history, insight. Never anything more than a hint at a deeper story. Never more. Leave it mysterious. Saying this, it was as if Maddox had reached into a top hat and between his fingers extracted and presented her a world inside a marble. Transformed in an instant into a completely different person. TING! Pop! Voila! *That's me now!*

THURSDAY EVENING

I teach creative writing to grown men and women at the adult education center in Boston. Each semester I meet a new batch of humans—who work, who have jobs, have families, responsibilities, commutes, bills, matching dinner plates, landlines, sick relatives, dreams. They come to me to fetch a piece of their brains that has gone missing.

"I am just in a rut and need to do something completely different than what I do at the law office."

"I used to write in a journal, poetry, when I was in high school, and I haven't in so long that I need someone to give me due dates so that I get into it again."

"I just need to try something new, get my creative juices flowing."

"My wife made me sign up."

And on and on. All the same story. Everyone needs to kick-start their creative half. I imagine the day that I finally interview for a cubicle job and say: *"I just need to get into a rut, I am being too creative."* And it's true. The 'rut' they talk about sounds so desirable, so appropriate—what I should be doing. They are all able to make it. All able to work. What dedication! But they all seem to complain about losing part of themselves in the process. I try my best to inspire them. I got a grandfather who hadn't read a book since high school to buy a collection of short stories by Ernest Hemingway. He loved it! I felt that I earned a vacation that day. Vacation from what?

I can't imagine, though, how anyone figures that the act of creative writing is not a rut, is not hard, is something inspiring.

Tonight we are discussing a published short story that I had photocopied and distributed last week. I have prepared what I will say about the short story: its structure and detail; its character's arc and language. I know what these people won't know is going on behind the scenes here. It's not intelligence, not skill. It's experience. I can only tell them what has happened within me, what I've noticed, over so many years of reading this particular story, inferring what I infer because of my own years of writing a particular story. We only have one to tell, and we try a boatload of ways to tell it.

Easy, if useless.

MINI LECTURE TO MY STUDENTS

[REPEATEDLY WHEN I GET TEACHING GIGS]

Invariably, someone asks, "Can you [one] get better at this [writing stories]?"

Which prompts my mini lecture:

"People are born with certain abilities, talents, at various levels for various things. Remember the story we read by David Foster Wallace, 'Forever Overhead'? Well, that guy was born with a certain brain that is better than yours, mine. He was born with intellectual talent. 'Gifted.' Now, take my mother. I love her to death, but she has never written a story in her life. If she started working on a story today, and she finished an arduous draft in six weeks—complete but rough draft of one story in six weeks—if she did that, and then she, every single day, for one hour, for one year, reworked that one story, then by the end of that regiment she would have an amazing story. This is both a comfort and a source of embarrassment and fear: anyone can write a good story. Anyone! And I apologize to my mother for making her the example of an 'anyone,' but she would acknowledge that she has not formally studied writing or formally read like an English Major.

"So, isn't it a comfort in that anyone can write a story, given they put in the time? Yes! Isn't it a source of embarrassment that you can dedicate your time to story writing when anyone could do it if they put in the practice? The thing is that what makes a writer good is practice. Like anything else. The thing that makes a successful writer so cool is that no one can imagine putting in that much practice. How many of you write for one hour every day? See? If you did? Do you know what you could do? Dream big. But none of you are going to do that. I know it. It is just too hard to write every single day for an hour. That's why those people who become successful writers are so revered. We know, inherently, that they did what we could not (not that they have a god's-gift that we don't but that they had a dedication we didn't (or a means)). They had someone supporting them. Maybe they had a trust fund? Who knows!? All it is is *practice*. But practice is the fucking hard part. Like anything else.

"So, my mom and DFW start writing a story on the same day. They finish a rough draft on the same day. They both then spend one year revising that story, and they finish the final draft on the same day. What do they have?

"What my mother has: a great story, better than I could write, because there's no way in Hell I'm spending a full year on a single story. It's a great story. Good job, Mom. You put in the time. You probably tried it all before you reached the final product. You allowed for experimentation in the middle and came to a serene finale. Applause applause.

"What DFW has: a story so good that the paper on which it's written turns to tissues in your shaking hands while you weep a strangely complex weep of a mingling between deep personal sadness and complicated distinctly American sadness. A showstopper.

"But all of us can have an excellent story, if we put in the practice. So, yes, one can get much better at this. We are all given words. By contrast, we are not all given leaping ability, racquet speed, accuracy, hand-eye coordination. We can improve at tennis, but only to the max of our physical ability. With writing, we can go anywhere. There's that guy, you know, the guy with 'locked-in syndrome' who wrote a book that was really good. You don't need to hit a 140 mph serve to do this shit. You just need to do this shit. But some of us will choose not to. Why? Because it's actually not that cool to be a writer. It's all practice. We are practicing our whole lives for some match with some *thing* some *where*. The writing practice may not even be preparing you for writing. It may be preparing you for your life."

[then some god speaks through me]

"Just write every day. I guarantee you'll make it.

"Just try everything out. If you try every way to be sad, then you'll figure it out: you'll perfect your grief. It's just practice. You'll feel it someday. Do anything for as long as it takes. If you write your story in every possible fictional way, you'll understand your loss. I promise."

When I exit my trance, everyone's still in the room with me. Oh no.

THURSDAY LATE EVENING

I get a drink after teaching. Every week. Downtown Boston is crummy for decent bars. It's all suits and stuffy staff all over. Nowhere to go in jeans and a tee and not feel weird classism for at least a moment. This week, I go to the lounge inside the old Ritz Carlton. Elegant and shit. I like its reliable dimness. Highlights of a college football game play on the television. I try to read the names of the teams, see if there's any reason to care about the numbers next to them. But I can't see any of the details on the screen. Damn weird Stargardt's eye disease. I order a Bud. Figure it's the cheapest. It is. It isn't cheap.

My friend, Lester, he called his degree in English Literature from a very good liberal college in Oregon a "One hundred thousand dollar book club." It's not nonsense. And my degree! It was a book club that didn't even read the canon; we wrote the stuff.

I polish off the beer. Get another.

A professor of mine, at the writing school in the desert, he told us: "Don't ever tell someone next to you on the plane that you're a writer when they ask you what you do. Tell them you're anything but that."

My dad would have said: "I'm a doctor." That basically explains it and impresses. Maybe.

I eat the assortment of pretzels and nuts in the tray before me. Polish off the second bud, ask to see a cocktail menu.

There are so many books at my apartment. I could hoist up my mattress and box spring on their spines. I could sit on benches of books. I could build a dinner table of perfect-bound pages. A coffee table of texts. A counter and chopping block of pages and words. A bookshelf of books.

Could I build a person of books? A living thing with all the pages and words?

I pay for the drinks and walk through the Boston Public Gardens to the parking garage under the Boston Common to get inside my car made of I don't know what.

FATHER'S BOOKS AND WRITINGS

[FIVE YEARS AFTER]

Milo's love of books began after his father exploded. At the private high school he was attending, the students read classics—*The Odyssey*, *The Iliad*, *The Aeniad*, Shakespeare plays, and on and on. But Milo wasn't a huge fan until senior year (months after Dad went POP!) until he read Knut Hamsun's *Hunger*, Fitzgerald's *The Great Gatsby*, Hemingway's *The Sun Also Rises*, Flaubert's *Madame Bovary*, Salinger's *Nine Stories*, Brett Easton Ellis' *The Informers* and *American Psycho*, Mann's *Death in Venice*, Calvino's *If on a Winter's Night a Traveler*, David Foster Wallace's *Girl with Curious Hair*, Twain's *The Adventures of Huckleberry Finn*, Carver shorts, Mansfield, Chekhov, Chopin, LeGuin, Poe, and more and more—it was only after his father died that he 'discovered the world of books.' At the same time, Milo started writing and thinking that he was different than his father. Milo himself was into literature, he thought. Art was cool—this happened within him. He was drawn to it, maybe the way his father was drawn to science. They were different, in a classic way, and Milo would reconcile this at some point down the road. He thought he would. With practice. He felt it.

When Milo moved into his first apartment after college, he went into the basement of his parents' house to look for whatever he could sit on, put coffee mugs on, whatever furniture he could steal from the cellar. Milo discovered a bookshelf in a dark corner. A THOUSAND BOOKS! Jesus Christ, what a bounty! It was all there—all the books in the world, or at least all the necessary ones. Jules Vern, Conrad,

Tolstoy, Dostoyevsky, Twain, Hugo, Shakespeare, Hemingway, Maupassant, Proust, Wolfe, Woolf, Wolf, Kerouac, Miller, Austen, Steinbeck, Dante, and on and way on. All of them in tiny print, in mass paperback. His dad had read them—the whole canon, it turned out. And, because his father had no money when he was young and studying, he got these mass-market copies, copies Milo can barely read because of the eye disease and all. This moment—down in the basement, staring at his books, all these books that Milo had read or that were on his list, staring at this world of words that his father had lived in, Milo imagined his dad in his tiny studios while attending medical school, in his shared dorm rooms at Springfield College, in his hammocks in the Navy, at night, alone, quietly reading, enjoying this world of adventure and escape—his father lived it. He loved it. He must've loved it—nobody Milo knows who isn't a writer or lit student reads this much. It was a moment that deeply, deeply saddened him.

He pulled a book off the shelf, perfectly dusty and rigid. He wiped the cover: *Vanity Fair*. The exact size and stiffness of a brick in his hand. Dead. Milo wanted it to live. Wanted it to speak. Wanted to open the book and find musical notes. Wanted his dad to tell him what he thought of these, why he read them, why he hadn't written, what was this? Milo thought his dad had one-upped him: he had become a doctor while at the same time putting the entire syllabus of ten English PhDs under his belt. How on earth did he do it? Why on earth hadn't he talked to Milo about books? Why only sports?

Milo took them all to his new place in Cambridge. He didn't read them—the print. But he did touch them. Picked them up and said, 'my dad read this.' He told himself this. He thought, when he did read them (larger print versions) that his dad and he were in the same place, sharing something. They are father and son, after all, and when Milo got delighted, when Milo got drawn into a story, his father must've gotten carried to here, as well. It was weird and sad.

It felt weird. It's the only word for it.

Despite the weirdness, Milo felt grateful to authors, to these books, to these good books, for doing something within him that he'll reconcile at some point. With practice.

Also, Milo has heard tell of a journal that his father wrote in while living in Ecuador, but he hasn't asked to read it, yet. The tell he hears of is that it is phenomenal. He'll get to it.

However, the one poem he's read of his dad's is, frankly, crap.

TENNIS

[MOMENTS BEFORE]

I kneel by the bench at the side of the sky blue hard court to retie my sneakers with two big looped double knots, synched tight. I remove my wedding ring and Ironman watch, thread the gold ring over the band and secure the metal fastener. I flip the watch and ring combo into the outer zippered compartment of the gray racquet bag, slide the thing under the bench. I crack open a can of PENN tennis balls, like opening a can of Mountain Dew, just larger, more hollow, still green, and smelling kind of the same, chemical green fuzz, pins and needles in the nose. I stand and pocket the three balls. I tug at the fifty-pound test strings on the Prince Thunderstick; they squeak and crackle as they move into a more perfect parallel grid on the racquet face. They look straight enough. I fish the vibration softener from my pocket and weave it in between the two center strings at the bottom row. I slam the face against my palm five quick times, like breaking in a baseball glove, bouncier. The racquet's feeling good, strong, in tuned-up working order. The grid of strings burns my palm, brings up the blood inside me to form a red tic-tac-toe board on the ball of my thumb. Then stretch the quads, windmill the serving arm, windmill the off shoulder, roll the neck, a little jog to the center of the net. I measure it for regulation—stand the Thunderstick on the court, hold the place where the head ends with my pointer finger, flip the Thunderstick sideways: it fits from pointer finger to the top of the tape. Good and prepared. Smack the net cord to gauge tension. A *thwap*. It's pulled tight, locked at either end by heavy cranks. The court's inside a massive blue tent, ten tennis courts long, all separated by fifty-foot black nylon nets to catch errant forehands and backhands and mishits. The room is echoey, loud without content. I can hear the blasting of serves, clanging and echoing of racquets, unintelligible curses and exaltations from the matches all the way down the enormous courtroom.

Hutch, my doubles partner, is done fixing his request strings, jogging to the net. I point to the baseline; I'll serve. I stroll to the server's line, punching a tennis ball with my Thunderstick the whole way. At the baseline, I slam the ball into the court, and it leaps up over my head. It reaches its zenith, pauses, and drops back down. I snag it from the air.

Hutch looks to me from the box, and I just gesture for him to get ready. He turns. I wave with my racquet to Connell and Gates. They get organized. Gates is taking my serve, and Connell jogs to the box at the net.

I slide my toe to the white line. Lean over. Bounce the ball just inside the court. One. Two. Three. I grip the ball. Drop my right arm. Raise up my left. Push the ball up. Bend my knees. Toss the ball. Spring up. Raise my right arm. Bend elbow. Uncoil tricep. Push with my calves. On toes. Leave the ground. Rise up. Reach. Racquet face collides with ball at apex.

I hear the pop of contact. I feel the near imperceptible resistance of the light air-filled rubber ball against the strings. The finger snap of released tension. I hear the pop of the serve.

But then I'm not there. I see my racquet dropping to the baseline, hitting on its square on its head, bouncing, flipping, and rattling to a halt. I see Hutch looking to where I am, stunned. Connell and Gates are upright, not ready for the point as the ball sails by. They're moving toward the net with racquets down, mouths open. I look to my hands, only smoke rising up. Everything getting smaller, farther away, as I float up. Up to the rafters. Up to the ceiling. They're meeting at the baseline, picking up my racquet, looking all around. I hear them curiously calling my name, and it echoes and mixes with the noises from other matches. I continue up through the blue tent. It's twilight in June. I see the tennis club buildings lain out before me. The parking lot. Then the highway, all the red and yellow little car lights headed home to families, headed back from tennis, headed to their little living lives. I see the string of trails through the Blue Hills. I see my house. A light is on in the room above the garage. All like a peaceful model of small town life. Then it's too small. Then it's too dark. And then it's getting very cold. There was so much I still wanted to do. And then nothing.

GRAVE VISITS

[HARD TO TELL WHEN BUT DEFINITELY AFTER]

"It's nice," I say, nodding generally at the day or the green grass. A gentle slope of manicured lawn. A smooth, hilly, green and blue place, this cemetery. It's uninterrupted by headstones, all plaques in the ground. It tricks you. It's just a rolling heaven field.

"What?" my mom asks several seconds later. She's staring down at the grave plaque.

"Nothing," I say, forgetting what I meant.

FRIDAY EVENING

I have no interest in dancing tonight. Some people do.

"I am having a French night," I tell anyone who calls me to go out partying.

What a French night is:

I buy two bottles of Merlot, though the color is currently second on the list of my favorite wine colors, and it's seventh on the list of my favorite wines overall. I buy Brie. I buy a Baguette. I buy plenty of Bali Shag tobacco. I put on my red bandanna. I plan on drinking all the wine, eating all the baguette and Brie, smoking a heroic amount of cigarettes, listening to futuristic punk and dance tracks. All while sitting in front of the keyboard and typing so fast and hard that I vanish into whiteness. In there. It resembles France. In there. In the story I am writing so fast.

Ernest Hemingway wrote: "A young man who travels to Paris will take Paris with him wherever he goes, for Paris is a moveable feast." I read *A Moveable Feast*, the posthumously published account of Hemingway's times in Paris as a young man and young writer, just before I myself moved to Paris in the year 2002. It was one of those very perfect things. To read that, and go to the bookstores he visited. The parks where he killed pigeons and ate them because he was just so damn poor. But I didn't have an F. Scott Fitzgerald to compare my dick size with and show my stories to. I didn't have a Gertrude Stein to inspire and push me. I was missing something by that point in my life. What I did have was Merlot, cigarettes, loud music, and a red bandanna, which I wore at the keyboard most nights while typing so fast and hard that I disappeared. I found that.

Tonight is a French Night, and I will go away.

PARIS

[THREE YEARS AFTER]

In his twenty-first year Marshall lived in Mont Matre in a studio apartment with views of his neighbors' studio apartments, and he wrote story after story with characters based on his friends and family who were all thousands of nautical miles away in America. He missed them, and this was his way to be with them. Marshall submitted a story to an English literary journal published in Paris. He knew no one back home would ever see it. The story was called, "The Night Before Marshall's Dad Vanished." It was the actual account of what happened the night before his dad died.

This nonfiction under the guise of fiction was not accepted. But the editor asked to get an espresso with Marshall to discuss the piece. They never did get that espresso. The two of them fell off the face of the planet at exactly the same time—never wondering, never guilty, and falling. The journal was called Kilometer Zero and one could purchase it at Shakespeare and Company. Marshall's not sure if it exists anymore.

You see, Marshall's brother wouldn't allow him to write about the death of their father. When Marshall did muster the courage to show him a piece that referenced the death, his brother said: "Good. You really exploited our pain. Good job." That was when Marshall was in writing school in the desert. So he wrote and submitted these stories behind his back, behind a lot of backs, for a long while.

"The Night Before Marshall's Dad Vanished"
by
Marshall

"Tonight's the night." Marshall slapped his friend hello and congratulations for graduating high school. A horrible school for elitist kids outside Boston. Shirt and tie and all that. It was that sort of a place. "Tonight is most likely the night."

Walking out of the massive tent on the school's soccer field, Marshall and his newly graduated friend smiled. He teased a lot but he was actually sad to know that this boy was going away to Colorado College while he would be staying at that horrible school for yet another year. But they were smiling because tonight they would have a goodbye gathering. "Be there whenever you want." Marshall was referring to his parents' house where the makeshift party would be held. "I'll prepare the place." And that meant that he would obtain certain drugs that he was still somewhat fond of. Speed mostly, painkillers too, and alcohol. He patted his friend on the back and saluted him. Everything was already nostalgic. "The beginning, not the end, remember that," Marshall shouted as he got into his mother's old car to drive home and make certain phone calls.

"Well yeah... I mean they told me that it is our night tonight. They will go to sleep and let us be in the loft." The loft was a converted attic above Marshall's garage. Not actually a loft, but it was the kids' room to hang out and sneak cigarettes into. "No. They don't care. They know that Stan graduated today and that we all need to have a night. So it is here. No worries. Just come." Marshall was talking to his friend Lester who would also be remaining at the horrible shirt and tie institution for another year. Lester said he would be there. It was settled.

Stan arrived midday, sun still out and blinding him as it reflected in Marshall's pool. He tipped his ten-gallon hat to shade his eyes and turned slowly to Marshall, who was lounging in a chair. A lounge chair. "What did you get?"

"The usual. Dex and Ritalin and some Percocet. And beers."

"Can't believe it." Stan sat down at the edge of the pool, rolled up his tattered jeans, removed his sandals and slipped his feet under water.

"How's that?"

"I'm done with that place. Never to return as a student. I mean I've been there so long. I don't know anything but those damn hallways." Stan was serious.

"I know what you mean." Marshall did not know what Stan meant. "I'm sad you're going." Marshall was serious, too. He leaned forward and put his white T-shirt back on his skinny body, sticking with sweat to the back of the chair. Everything was slow and they were both aware of this. Marshall knew he was looking at a boy he might not see for god knows how long, a boy he had seen everyday, for the most part. The conversation was sparse and revolved mostly around disbelief. "Lester's coming tonight."

"Good. Good." And the two swam lazily for a half hour before toweling off and smiling genuinely.

Empty beer bottles, cigarettes, and clothes painted the loft a Monet of greens and oranges. Moved into the center of the room, the Ping-Pong table doubled as a stepladder to the roof and a flat surface to snort lines of speed off. The residual blue powder on the table, the blue snot from their young noses, all just innocence. CD jewel cases and silver discs sprinkled the area near the stereo. The TV glowed with infomercials for weight loss. They were on the roof looking at stars.

"I hate to do this. But I mean I don't, too. Those stars. They just get me sometimes." Stan was a hippie.

"Hippie." Marshall was kidding.

"No those stars...I don't know. They just make me seem small."

"We are small." This comment came matter-of-factly from Marshall's mouth. "We're tiny little things." He didn't actually know where he was headed with that statement so he cracked his back and continued in a different vein. "I love this roof. I remember when this loft was built. This one day, when I was younger, my parents opened the door and showed me and my brother the space they had made for us. Before we all fucked it up, the rugs were white and the walls were white. Clean." Marshall paused and looked back through the skylight to the loft, surveying its present status. "But that is great, too. We've used it, you know? We've come up here for years and used it. And now you're taking off. You're leaving for a long time and we're all here tonight again." Marshall stopped his speech because he noticed how drunk it sounded. He took a pull of his beer and picked some dirt off his bare foot.

"I see that." Lester sounded sad. "I love coming here and most of my memories are from this place. Coming here and drinking and smoking and whatever else. It is a gift. I think I'm going to write your mom and dad a note. Just saying how thankful I am to be at your house so much."

Lester did write a note to Marshall's mom later, but with a different type of message.

"We can make as much noise as we want and my parents never hear." He lit a cigarette. He threw his bottle at an oak. It exploded. "I think I'll write my mom a letter, too."

They all laughed. The three of them. Smiling about their little friendship and more quietly about how much they were going to miss each other. Young Marshall and his two young friends looked at each other, on a roof at night.

The next day: POP!

The entire concept is the simple juxtaposition of the title and the account thereafter. The hope is that one reads the account with a death lens. It's a straight rip off of a story Marshall had never actually read but heard about: "Days Before No One Heard from [So-and-

So] Again". Something like that. Marshall can see now, though, that writing this story is insane. Writing this and never showing it to anyone, trying to publish in a foreign land's small literary magazine. There are clearly things that Marshall wanted to talk about, wanted to feel. But he deflected, continuously, into shit stories like this, hoping that someone would read it and throw him on their back and carry him off to wherever you take broken things for healing. But no one ever did. And no one, rightfully, wanted to publish the juvenilia.

Look: The thing is:

Marshall doesn't want to encase his father's death in artifice, but in order to tell it effectively, to convey the emotions in any palpable sense he must angle it so. The truth is: the story's real goal, the real change we're reading and writing for here will happen in Marshall; the epiphany-what-have-you will POP when he puts the pen down; it will strike when he stops trying to convey a feeling that he doesn't even understand yet; and, instead, he just talks to someone about it. So, here, today, Marshall would like to put the telling of it in story form to bed, turn to whoever's around, and say, "

But he can't yet. He can't tell it straight. He can't look right at it. He's just not ready. Not yet. Soon.

SATURDAY MORNING

I have torn the shades off my windows.

Light blasts in through two skylights, one of which is directly over my bed, through two ratty old windows on either side of the apartment that the management company has yet to replace. I need this. I would sleep forever without the daylight. I fight the inevitable descent into October's mysterious depression with this and other arbitrary tricks.

But I don't get right up today. I think that on Wednesday I have to go to this bereavement group and help a young kid who's lost his father. I don't get cynical when I say 'lost' in my head, because I am questioning a lot of things right now. I have no idea what to say to this kid. No clue how to help. Even if I was sure that no one can truly help, I have no idea how to interact with anyone who has lost someone, for I don't know really what it's like.

I am sure that I am not the one to help this kid, thinking about how I've dealt so far. Have I dealt with anything? I have avoided therapy. Never read a touching book about loss that touched me touchingly. It is as if I am still waiting for my dad to die. This strikes me as weird. Leads me to believe that instead of being asked to help this kid, that my mother and her friends and my friends and our relatives have all gotten together behind my back to discuss me and how I haven't actually handled the loss at all. I am unemployed and still dreaming of being a writer. Something's way more than amiss. I feel left behind by the world, and maybe someone finally, benevolently said, "He hasn't handled it well, let's have an intervention." Why else would my mother ask me to do this? She doesn't have a clue as to how I've dealt with the loss! We haven't discussed it in so long that we've forgotten that it is apparent every single day that we are fucked up. I fear that I will arrive at this meeting and the whole thing will be an elaborate ruse to get me into therapy. I have gotten nowhere. Maybe they will help me. Carted away in new white clothes.

But, just in case it isn't an intervention and I am actually supposed to help this kid, I think about how I have dealt with this. Through writing. Through stories. These are the only therapy sessions I've taken, in a way. The only person I've talked to about death is the white bull. It's been easier because I have a mask on. A visiting writer and editor to the writing school in the desert said: "I can get closer to the truth in my fiction, because I can hide behind the label of fiction. In nonfiction, I change things, because everyone knows it's true." Of course! When you tell someone that your friend has a problem with such-and-such a thing, it is easier to say what is bothering you! My fiction has been my call for help? Is it a call for help, and now someone has finally answered and I am to have myself whisked away to an insane asylum? Twenty-seven is the last age at which people discover they have schizophrenia. Maybe I discover that I have been a psycho, never admitting to being fucked up when it is so obvious. Or looking so normal when I shouldn't. I couldn't. But I do?

What have I done to deal? What could I possibly impart to this little fucked up high school kid, who probably is dealing with it normally by appearing so fucked up? I should have been crazy in high school. But I kept my nose down, studied, did well, applied to colleges and really cared about which one I would get into. I joined groups. I maintained a relationship with a girl, kept my friends laughing. All that shit. So, someone finally noticed that I didn't bring a gun to school, and that meant that I was even more— paradoxically— fucked up than everyone else who lost a parent.

Oh heavens me!

FEBRUARY 20TH, 2009

[ELEVEN YEARS AFTER]

I am no believer. Extremely recently, something caused me to reinforce this rigid belief.

I have finished a rough draft of this very book. October has passed. The bereavement meeting is in the past now. I have been writing since last July, this very story. I began reworking part of it after October.

Yesterday, I wrote a period that marked the end, a satisfactory stopping point to allow myself the chance to take the whole rough thing in and begin editing. Yesterday I taught my creative writing class to grown-ups. Last night, something very strange happened. But I am no believer.

Leaving class, before checking my voicemails and texts, I decided that I would not go out and meet up with Carl, if he was even wanting that. I was not going to meet up with Anna, if the same thing happened. I resolved to go home and look at this very story. I felt a feeling that I have never felt before: I wanted to be *with* the story, just be in its company as if it were a person. I wanted to spend time with it, because lately I'd felt the story had begun a dialog with me. It was becoming a two-way conversation, and it was as if it could provide good company. I needed to allow it that chance to communicate with me. I actually pictured printing this very story and placing the stack of papers next to me on the couch or in my bed, cracking a beer and just sitting or lying with the pages. This was new, and I had prepared my speech to Carl and Anna: "This is going to sound very weird, but I just want to be with my story tonight." I pictured Carl's reaction, a mocking, but I was ready to withstand the laughs at my expense. I pictured Anna's brief affront—*is this really the lengths he'll go to, the excuses he'll now make to avoid being with me?* But it was true. I just wanted to allow this story to sit and live and breathe a little, see if it actually communicated something to me.

Guess what? Both Anna and Carl had called, left five messages, texted me ad nauseam and were together, somewhere in Boston. They never hang out together without me. It was impossible to say no. My best friend and my girlfriend had taken a step, reached out to one another, and then they wanted me to join in. For the first time. The awkwardness that my refusal would have caused was too much, so I said yes.

And of course it was fun. They wound up at my studio here in Cambridge. I eyed the computer and printer. I wanted to tell them that I just needed to be with the story, not alone, but with the story. But I did not. It was a weird feeling.

This morning we all breakfasted at a diner, and it was celebratory and fun and hung over and wonderful. When we all parted ways, Carl to his craziness, Anna to her appointments, I to my apartment and unscheduledness, I finally saw the date on the calendar: February 20th. Do you know what today is, besides the day after my first ever desire to be alone with an inanimate object that I believed to be becoming animate, besides the day after I finished a rough draft of a story called POP!, which is a double entendre, signifying at once both my dad and his death?

Today is my dad's birthday.

I am no believer, and I fucked myself by not giving into believing last night.

So I will play Writer's Ouija, leaving my fingers on the keyboard, waiting for an apparition to move the keys. "Use my fingers," I say. Tell me a story.

UNRELENTING PEN PAL

[PERIODICALLY AND WITHOUT WARNING AFTER]

Pen pals. What the fuck? In third grade, everybody in class got assigned a pen pal. Mine lived somewhere in the middle of the country, and I remember reading the word "tractor" in the one letter I received from him. In my one letter, I made up mostly every detail, just blatantly lying to the kid, wanting to entertain not connect. The relationship failed. And with that, I thought my days of pen palling were finished.

Say you first meet someone face to face, then you correspond with that person solely through the post, never laying eyes or ears or hands on him or her ever again: does this person earn the title of pen pal? If so, then I have had more pen pals since third grade: female, short-lived, and horny.

When I was twelve and in Disney World, I met a girl my age by the pool of the hotel, The Yacht and Beach Club, which is, incidentally, a sweet hotel with a ridiculously enormous pool with sand on the floor, a slide that is actually hollowed out of a ship's mast, and a current that cruises through the entirety. I forget her name, but we chatted about the pool and the slide and music. Then she asked for my mailing address. That was that, I thought. But then, one day a letter arrived at my parents' house, addressed to me. The handwriting was large and respectful of the lines and margins. The tone was warm and curious, but it was not from that girl I met by the pool. No! It was from her sister!

This girl's sister had come to the conclusion that her younger sister was fond of me and wanted to reconnect with yours truly, perhaps romantically this time around. But she was too nervous to write. The older sister took the matter into her own hands, acting as matchmaker. Can you imagine? Being so timid as not to be able to even write a letter? Well, I was being asked in the letter to write to the girl in question. Here's the mailing address, and so forth. I did write. I made up a lot of stuff, mailed it off, and that was that. It's hard to maintain a relationship that begins with dishonesty. Even harder when the relationship lacks every form of contact save for written words. It's really hard to make out with someone in letters, not to mention awkward with all the mailmen there. It's hard to touch someone with only written words. So, I thought, I had my second chance and blew it.

Years of a pen pal-less life rocketed by.

Then! One day I received a letter from someone I'd never met. Addressed to me! The tone was retrospective, intimate. This person was instantly, from sentence one, much more complex than my previous pen pals. His first letter was about how he had become recently observant of his observations of his friends; he had leapt from casually noticing his friends' mannerisms and speech quirks to defining them as characters in a story, shaping whole worlds in their heads while hanging out, instead of just enjoying life. He wished to retrieve the purity he felt in interacting with some of them, the purity of withholding a potential story idea. He wanted to live in the moment. He wrote that he was sensing that his best friend's girlfriend was developing a crush on him, and this made him uncomfortable around the two, so he withdrew. It was so weird! So gloriously weird and shocking to receive.

I didn't write to him. And I thought that would be the end of it. A person writing to another in hopes of beginning a pen pal relationship does not ask twice.

But then! One day I got an email from the same guy. The jist of it was that he was extremely confused: he wasn't sure if he was being good, or if he should even ask that of himself, or if he knew what good even was anymore. He cited recent examples at being bad, just simply inconsiderate moments. He cited recent attempts at being good, holding the door for people. He was down and out and going in circles.

Again, I didn't reply, and I wasn't sure where this relationship was headed.

Then, one morning I woke up, reached into the pocket of the jeans I had fallen asleep in and extracted a folded up letter. The handwriting was atrocious: letters of all different sizes, no respect for the lines or margins, just terrible, barely legible. The only line I could make out was "No one thinks about my dad..."

I didn't reply. I wanted no more of these notes.

But they just kept coming, and he didn't limit himself to text communication:

I'd wake up to find my four track on, playing a loop of very weird music he'd recorded in the night—all arrhythmic minor chords. Wake up to find an entire roll of film he'd shot, ready to be developed. Wake up and see an email on my desktop addressed to DAD@HEAVEN. ORG. Find notes scrawled over bar receipts. Computer printouts taped all over my bedroom, reading: "Insert inspiration here" twenty thousand times. Broken plates. Cigarette burns. Bruises and cuts on my face. My fist swollen into a spearoid, unclenchable for days. Blood. Fire. Bent bones. He has tried and continues to try every way under the sun and the moon to get my attention.

But I can't write back. I just receive all this stuff, note it, and quietly continue on. I simply can't write him. I don't know what I'd say. Plus, I have no idea where he lives.

SUNDAY AFTERNOON

I can only imagine for now what my closest friend is doing anyway.

There's another guy. Lester. He is currently up in Maine, northern Maine, working for a woman named Billy. He sleeps in a tent on the farm. Every day he wakes up at dawn to an actual rooster's call and tends the fields. He pulls weeds. He moves the chicken cart twenty feet over so that the chickens, soon to be slaughtered, will have a new area of grass to eat and new space to shit on. He opens the hencoop and allows them to roam and lay eggs in a hay-filled basket. He fills up a bag with peaches and rhubarb to make wine. He has been doing this for six months now, and I haven't seen him since he left.

Lester is my best friend, and, along with my oldest friend, the three of us: Lester, Carl, and I are all doing very different work. Work that no one thought we'd be doing. All work that we have chosen for strange reasons. Lester doesn't care about being a farmer; he needed to do something, needed to feel pain, the pain of work. Carl doesn't need to stay up until the sun rises, reading on the Internet, or fix and remodel computer circuits till he's bleary-eyed. I don't need to wake up and write and get stressed all day about it. We could just choose to be happy, have normal jobs. We're simply not cut out for it. This is marvelous. Marvelously strange.

What are we searching for? What are we so afraid to face?

Lester will be done with the farm gig in a week, come here to visit me, tell me stories. I will go to the bereavement group. Carl will tough it out and meet us during the day, without sleeping through it. We'll debrief each other and try our best to understand. Then we'll go back to our weird duties. Someday, I hope, we will get together and say: I found it! It's out there. The search, the going out, the all of that matters. Or at least it's a good story.

WRITING WORKSHOP

[SEVEN YEARS AFTER]

The first story Murphy wrote after moving to the desert to "study" creative writing at the MFA program was originally titled "The Perfect Goodbye" and was about saying *see ya in a few years* to everyone in his Boston world. Of course, it had a reference to his dad, a nod of sorts to a non-thing, that sensible void whom he was leaving behind as well. He honestly felt tethered to these people but borne toward his own personal goal of writing, which has always coexisted with the absence of loved ones. This was a private journey to the act of writing, to a desert, a place that could actually be any-damn-where. The story is surreal. An unnamed narrator is setting up a thirteen-rung ladder in the middle of a bright green field. Mountains in the distance. He is asking for the help of his three friends and his mother. He wants to climb the thirteen-rung ladder, and swing from a rope, anchored in the sun, to launch himself over the mountains. It's a suicide-farewell type thing.

Excerpt: "Ready Set"

Mom, I need you to be prideful now. Prideful, remember. You're thinking of me getting on the bus for the first time in kindergarten. You're saying goodbye to me, going off to do the ten hundred things I've done and that you've eased me into, worried, but prideful, remember. Your face is aglow with tears of joy—this is my destiny. Picture me —here, look through the frame I'm making with my fingers—draped in medals on center stage inside a stadium that is so grand that the dome scrapes clouds, and it is full up, all full up with fans, reverent students, professors, government officials, news teams, and they are all hushed, waiting for me to speak to them, but all I do is thank you, Mom. Thank you, Mom—you were the one who got me here—without you, I couldn't have dreamed of all this… and all that. You love it. Your little boy is a man. And you've always got something on me because when the milkman came, and I opened the door, and he handed me the bottle of milk when I was, like, three, I dropped it and it shattered on our foyer floor and I cried, feeling that I'd done something wrong, and you comforted me, explaining that it was OK. You were a little taken aback by my reaction, but you taught me that lesson that so many people don't understand. Move on. No use crying. Unless the tears are triumphant, prideful like you are conjuring now. Good. Good dress, too, Mom—simple, elegant, black. Your hair is catching the wind very nicely. Good. The lines on your face are all the years I owe you. I will get it all, and I will give it back to you. Know this. Perfect. Stay there, a little behind the crowd of my friends: Lester, Carl, and Laura. You can easily take a step back and let me go. Perfect. Hold it.

And last night we did it right, guys. I'll pause on the third rung to say this. Last night, the night before I leave, we just sat around with some beers on the kitchen floor, backs resting against emptied cabinets and emptied drawers, looking over photos with turned up edges, laughing, and telling stories. No one mentioned what we all knew: I'm gone in a day. We just wanted one more night of goodness. And it was. I'll touch my heart now to show you all that I'm serious, that I'm touched. Another good night to take along with me. Lester doing that trick with his eyes, where it looks like they're gone, back in his head. Carl extinguishing everybody's cigarettes when he notices they're not quite out, always helping to see things through to their proper ends—snuffing them. Laura informing us of how the French philosophize our climaxes, and then faking an orgasm. Good work, friends. And, Mom, a last good home-cooked meal, simply your chicken and mashed potatoes, a joke about me eating more vegetables—did you really think you could convince me, even now? And Mattie begging for table food. Me giving it to her with a wink—I mean what could you do? I'm leaving. I can cheat a little. Then you sitting me down—serious for a moment—giving me a feather, mentioning how you have this thing about found feathers, which I never knew, all this time, something that has to do with Dad—that after he died, you started seeing feathers everywhere and collecting them—a shard of heaven. He's OK. We're OK, aren't we, Mom? Well, that feather is in my breast pocket, and if anyone asks about it—it's personal, it's family, it's a keepsake from my mom, and somehow, from Dad, too. Yeah, that's from Dad, too. And enough feathers make a wing. I'll believe in this with you, and it is good to believe in something spiritual, I think, now. Thank you. And for everything. For the good and the bad we shared. You were there. I hope I was there for you. A son who knows his mom like a grateful cub, like a friend when the leaves fall and nights end with embers. Fluttering. Up? Down? Let's go ahead and hear that fluttering.

Murphy was serious while writing that story. Murphy meant it, although it was fictional and exaggerated. The story had a tenderness, he thought, to these characters—all real people. But! All the workshoppers said it was sarcastic. Not a knock. But not the intention. And the author's intention has very little to do with the meaning of a story, Murphy tells his students, but no. Damn it. No. He loved these people. He wasn't sarcastic when he said *I love you*. And here is where Murphy began to learn that maybe he's an asshole? Is this where he did that?

He attempted to change the tone and switched the title to "The Director's Bow," hoping to make a fool of the protagonist and beacons of grace of the leave-letters. This didn't fix the problem, the tonal dissonance between page and heart. Murphy put the protagonist in a surreal setting, changed the title to "Borne." Them! He discovered a possible triple entendre if the title became "Bourne"—an archaic word for a boundary, an end. So, the sound of the word conjures two other possible meanings, all similarly defined, if you count antonyms as similar. Birth. Launch. End. Cool! But that sucked, quickly after the re-titling: it was either pretentious or going to straight miss, so Murphy changed it to "Ready Set."

Today, he's still reworking the story, and it is called "What Leave-Taking Malcolm Says!" He'll make sense of his father, he feels.

Some people see shrinks.

SAINT BUFFOON

[SIX YEARS BEFORE]

You never come across an obit for an asshole. Everyone is sainted when they die. Fair enough. There's no need to take a parting shot at someone when they're worm food. Major's dad was no exception.

So a saint exploded one night, and here Major was, this messed up kid, thinking he wasn't what a saint would have wanted to leave behind. In life, Major liked that he looked up to his father. In death, he was inspired to discover Dad's awfulness.

Major's own recollections of his father's shittiness are scant. And what he does have on brain-file isn't the stuff of evil, but it's all, just like, weird, humanizing, maybe. Here:

The closest arcade was at the Walpole Mall, a place called Dream Machine, where Major could satisfy his cravings for buttons, joysticks, computer images, gore, points, the weight of tokens in his palm, the potential transport they represented. So, his dad would take him sometimes. And, to occupy his time, Dad would play the pinball machines. Back then, Major thought pinball was lame. Now, he plays pinball machines. But that's not what he's getting at.

This one time, after Major had traded in one of his dad's five dollar bills for close to an hour of Street Fighter and Area 51 and one disappointing round of Pac Man, which he played only out of respect for the history of gaming, his dad and he strolled around the mall, ducking into sporting goods stores to scope tennis racquets, buy some string shock absorbers, a couple wrist bands, and cans of PENN tennis balls. All of a sudden, by the uninspiring mall fountain below the high skylights at the nexus of all hallways, a woman about Major's dad's age yelled, "Lee? Lee Polanzak?"

And Major got to watch as his father interacted with an old friend. It was the predictable catch-up chit chat, but what he'll always remember—what sticks with Major today more viscerally than the kindness and companionship of his father in those days when he took him to arcades and talked sports and was basically just being a great dad—is the moment when their small reunion was finished. The conversation ran its short course, and his father and this woman were about to part ways, and in place of the usual "Nice to see you" or "Take care" or even a terse but acceptable "Bye", Major's father put up his hand and formed a peace sign and said "Peace."

What the fuck was that?

That was no go-to sign off of his dad's. That was no moment of acknowledgement of the current war. There was no war. That was not a nostalgic gesture, recalling the way these two people used to say goodbye, like back when they were hippies or something. That was a straight up awkward, uncouth, social-anxiety-induced blunder. A fuck up.

Now, that's not awful, but Major thinks about it, and he allows himself to understand that his father was not all a med school diploma-having, Naval surgeon-being, NASA research team-belonging, patient life-saving, and tennis-playing saint. He was equally a fucking weirdo.

How strange. The moments, sound bites, and images that stick in the brain. Why does one lock in, grab hold, and pop up again and again. Things seemingly meaningless, but because of their frequency of recall becoming meaningful? Why? These things must matter.

Peace.

MONDAY AFTERNOON

"The meeting's tomorrow night"

"What? You said Wednesday."

"No, I said Tuesday night. Do you listen when I talk?"

"You said Wednesday."

"Well, it is tomorrow night."

"You told me."

"Mark!"

"Fine. But I just wish you hadn't screwed that up."

"Do you teach tomorrow?"

"No. Thursdays."

"Then you can come? You don't have plans do you?"

"No. I'll come. So what do I have to do? Come to your house by when?"

"Five thirty."

"Five thirty. OK. And we'll drive?"

"Yes."

"Do I have to wear anything, like a tie or something?"

"Look nice, please. Don't wear those tattered jeans."

"Fine. I just wish I could know things ahead of time."

"I told you."

"No, you didn't."

"And you have to talk."

"What?"

"You have to talk."

"Like share my story if I want?"

"No, you are a guest speaker."

"You said—"

"I told you, Mark. Now, come on!"

"You certainly did not tell me that I was a 'guest speaker.'"

"Mark!"

"What the hell! I thought I was going to go there and maybe. Maybe! Talk to a kid afterward. You haven't told me anything. Now I'm a speaker?"

"Can you just do this for me. I told you."

"Oh my god. You lied to me. You did. You lied to get me to agree to this. Now you've told people I'm agreeing to this. Now, you're telling me the truth."

"No I didn't. I did not lie to you. Don't call me a liar. I told you about this a week ago."

"You told me five days ago and said nothing about giving a speech."

"Just talk with the group of kids. Tell them your experience. It is good for them to hear from a young person who's been through this."

"You did not tell—Hold on, I have a another call—Hello? I'm on the other line with my mom. She lied to me... You know that bereavement group thing?... I am to be a guest speaker... Yeah!..... I can't believe this... She lied because she knew I wouldn't go... I'll call you back—Ma?"

Am I complaining or bragging? About the loss?

"Just be here at five thirty tomorrow."

"I can't believe this."

"Mark!"

"I don't believe it."

"Good bye."

PHONES

[HOURS AFTER AND ONGOING]

It's any midafternoon, and I'm bored. I call my brother to talk about the Celtics or an upcoming tennis tournament.

He answers, "Is everything okay?"

Or, directly after his hello but before talking, I declare: "No emergency."

Defibrillators were not standard in ambulances when my father exploded, but then again: there was no heart to jumpstart.

Defibrillators shoot 1,700 volts into the chest, the power of which can turn on a heart muscle that has been turned off. Like flicking on a light switch with a sledgehammer.

Phones ring when an encoded signal travels along a wire or through the air with a specific address of destination. When the signal reaches a phone in a house, ac current passes through copper, which changes the dc current from fifty volts to one hundred volts, which rattles a bell and makes the phone go BRIIING BRIIING!! Or flicks on a light switch and a recorded ringringring. Or cues a cell phone to play a digitized song. Or causes a light to flash in the houses of the deaf.

At any given moment, there is a phone ringing. At any given moment, there is a defibrillator ringing someone's heart.

If I hear a phone ringing, my heart rate increases. I get anxious. When I hear phones ring, I become terribly sad. I hate them. I have programmed a very upbeat song as the ring in my cell phone.

This helps a little. I used to have it set to simply beep, like an EKG machine. But slow. Never quick. Never one long beep either.

San Francisco, June 11, 1998. In a tiny apartment in Knob Hill, sitting on a shared balcony, my brother smokes a Marlboro Red with his roommate and old high school friend, Stewart. My brother has landed a job straight out of college, doing marketing. A good starter job. Stewart is working for a new website. They are twenty-three and happy. They stare at the sky, which is pinkish now, with a few swipes of royal blue. The sun is setting. Perfect weather.

The phone rings, and Stewart heads in through the slider to get it. My brother takes a drag, maybe he takes a sip of a beer. Free.

Canton, Massachusetts, June 11, 1998. I am asleep, or at least I am as still as the dead in my bed. My mother is downstairs in the family room with Dr. Brennen, who picked us up from the hospital. I have said that I am going to bed. If I just sleep, I think, then tomorrow will come without me having to do much more insane thinking and crying. My mother stays up with Dr. Brennen.

Eventually Dr. Brennen leaves my mother. She is to get into bed for the first time without her husband. But my mother cannot just go to bed and let the earth rotate around til tomorrow like me. She has to make a phone call to her first born on the other side of the country. She has to pick up the phone, dial the number of the apartment in San Francisco, where my brother now lives and is happy with his friend. She dials eleven numbers while sitting on her bed. She can hear the phone ringing in her ear. The encoded signal rockets along wires, over lakes, rivers, the great plains, the Rocky mountains, the desert, straight over other people in their houses making phone calls, over people sitting down for dinner in states and towns she's never been to, over cars on interstates. The signal charges along the metal conductors, racing from line to line, from tower to tower, leaping, sprinting, rolling, making its way to another ocean, carrying under its arm the breath of my mother, the message in her throat, streaking to the other side of the country, where it will cue the phone in my brother's apartment to ring, where it will cause a tiny electric current to create a circuit and jumpstart a ringing of bells, shock a machine, shock a heart, create a pulse.

HARMONY RUNS INTO
GERTRUDE AT THE MARKET

[UNKNOWN # OF YEARS AFTER]

It had been five years since Harmony had talked with Gertrude—one of her closest friends, the wife of one of her late husband's closest friends—when she spotted her picking over bananas at the local market. Gertrude had not noticed Harmony, Harmony noticed, and so she ducked behind a towering stack of potatoes.

She wasn't prepared for this.

Lately, Gertrude had not been present in Harmony's mind. No. Harmony had not even thought of the woman in *she didn't know how long* now. What a terrible thing to be reminded to remember this woman and what had occurred. But Harmony had moved on, forgotten the episodes. Now, Gertrude was no more than two fruit displays away, and Harmony felt her face heat up, her arms tingle. The hair follicles on her head suddenly had sensitivity. What to do?

Harmony peeked over the potatoes. Gertrude's hair was now almost completely white. Her face sagged. Her hands looked frail as she clutched a bunch of bananas. She was decaying, Harmony thought. Good. Then she ducked again. Good? Is that her real reaction to seeing this woman's loss of vitality? Was that the type of person she wanted herself to be? Someone who reveled in others' presumed unhappiness or misfortune or weakness? Certainly not, but she couldn't deny her initial reaction.

She thought back to times when Gertrude was on her mind nearly every day. She thought about what she wanted to say and never had said. What she wanted to do and never had done. Letters that were never written. Tell offs. Confusing tearful regrets. How did she finally feel about this woman? Where had she arrived in her feelings toward this close friend who was no longer a friend? Harmony admitted to herself that Gertrude was not even a factor anymore; it was as if Gertrude didn't exist anymore, hadn't existed, so gone from her mind was she. She peeked over the potatoes once more and watched Gertrude head to aisle thirteen—cereals and sodas.

Gertrude did not call Harmony, did not come by the house, and did not send cards in the two weeks that followed the funeral. Harmony finally drove to Gertrude's house, knocked on the door, and learned that she and her husband had gone out for brunch. When Gertrude then learned, upon returning from brunch that Harmony had stopped by, Gertrude called, apologized profusely, promised to be better from now on. But things did not get better. Gertrude did not right herself and support Harmony. She did not begin to come to the house with food or good company like so many others, so many less close friends did. Three more weeks went by without a call or visit. Harmony called Gertrude. The conversation was a repeat of the first. More weeks without Gertrude went by. Then, one day, the phone rang at Harmony's.

"Harmony, it's Gertrude. I am sending Amy over to pick up some snow tubes from your house. I remember you have snow tubes for floating in the pool, right? I'm sending Amy to come and borrow them."

And Amy, Gertrude's daughter, did come by to borrow Harmony's snow tubes. Amy sat in Harmony's living room, looked up at the high ceilings, the nice fireplace, and the nice floors, and she said: "I'd love a house like this. Are you going to sell it?"

Harmony gave over the snow tubes. She was not selling the house.

Then time just went by as it tends to do, and Gertrude's children graduated from things, married people, gave birth to people, and Harmony, never invited along, received cards from these children who still felt close to Harmony despite their mother's *whatever it was*. Harmony, still trying to figure out *whatever it was* or salvage the friendship over bad times, continued to make the calls that were never returned. Finally Gertrude said something to the effect of 'it was just so hard.' Just so hard to be around her friend who had lost her husband. So hard to be around hard times. What's harder, Harmony thought, was losing your husband, going through hard times and not having your friend. *More hard*. And she figured out that Gertrude was just selfish. She learned that Gertrude was having the time of her life while Harmony grieved, while Harmony leaned on the shoulders of less close friends who became more close friends through this time. Harmony gleaned that Gertrude couldn't have something hard in her life at that time, so she exited the hard friendship, opting for the easy stuff. Selfish, was the final conclusion Harmony had come to, and she couldn't believe it. She couldn't believe it daily for a long period of time. Her friend gave her up, gave up years of closeness, gave up, because she couldn't handle being strong in a time of need. Selfish.

But it had now been so long since she had thought of any of this. Here, in the local market confronted with this forgotten source of pain and anger, Harmony tried to remember if she had, in fact, ever prepared for this day, the day that they would meet again. Was there any revenge she had plotted? Or divine speech she had prepared. Or benevolence she had rehearsed? Anything ready inside her for this moment? She remembered wanting to say 'fuck you.' That was certainly in her, at least at some point, but no, that doesn't say it, does it? She remembered wanting to make a scene: run into Gertrude when Harmony herself was surrounded by friends and loved ones who were there for her, and then upon running into Gertrude, this crowd of good people would notice Gertrude, alone and weak, and Harmony would simply say, *oh, there's Gertrude, poor thing*, and she would say it loud, and her and her friends and loved ones would walk on. But that was going to be difficult to pull off considering Harmony was alone herself. Also, she didn't feel that strongly anymore. What was it now? What should she do? Do people need to be made aware of their wrongdoing? Or is that up to someone else? A higher power that would execute the proper justice? But Harmony was unclear on her beliefs of the afterlife and so forth.

Was it enough for Harmony to see that Gertrude was now an old woman? Her white hair and her boney hands and her still picking over bananas? Was that enough? To see this woman indeed become old and not look totally alive. Not look totally happy? Harmony was not sure.

She made her way to the cereal aisle.

Rounding the corner, Harmony spotted Gertrude down the aisle once more. Her heart rate quickened. She threw her hair back from her face, hair that had only a hint of gray. She drove her shopping cart before her as if it were a band of horses. She made herself taller. She breathed in. She puffed out her ample chest. Gertrude looked up the aisle, and the two met eyes. Had Gertrude prepared for this moment? Had she lost sleep, wondering what she'd say to Harmony if they ever clapped eyes on each other? Had she grappled with guilt or some such emotion?

Harmony beamed and strolled right up to Gertrude. Gertrude remained frozen with a box of cereal in her boney clutches. She had a slight hunch to her.

"Hello, Gertrude," said Harmony.

"Hello, Harmony," said Gertrude.

Harmony flipped her hair back. She felt athletic and alive. "How are you, Gertie?"

"Oh, I'm good. How are you, Harmony?"

"Oh." Harmony stared off, over the flowers by the registers, beyond the sliding doors of the market's exit, out to the blue day. She thought of starting a garden soon. Spring was approaching. She thought of her loved ones and how she hadn't thought of Gertrude in so so long now. She thought of the boundless opportunities in front of her for the rest of her life with or without her husband, with or without one of her close friends. Anything was possible, and no one had defeated her, she realized. She was as happy as ever. "Oh, Gertrude." Harmony returned her gaze to the hunched woman below her. "You know, I'm just awful," she beamed. "Things are just plain awful, and so hard."

This was not anything she had planned or prepared. This was something surprising. But today felt wonderful, and that was all that mattered for now. She pushed her cart on. She placed her groceries on the moving counter. She checked out.

THOUGHT AND MEMORY

[ALWAYS]

Usually you become aware that you've been playing a game only after a loss. But it's only a competition if you care about winning. In the game of Memory, there are no opponents. You can only lose if you play forever, meaning you never remember. But even a goldfish could eventually finish a match of Memory. Memory is used to test little kids sometimes when they are applying for advanced classes at a young age, or an advanced private school. Sometimes it is played for fun. Memory. It tests recall. Not knowledge. Not thought. Not creativity. Memories.

Your mother wanted you to go to a private school. Your dad was for public. Mom won. You found yourself playing Memory in a white room with an adult at some institution in the suburbs surrounding Boston.

Flip a card: an image of a blue cat. Now, you have the whole lot of down-turned cards in front of you and only one other blue cat. Flip another card: an image of a rose. Since they don't match, turn both cards face down. Flip a new card: a dog; flip another (the only way to lose this early is to flip the original cat or rose card again like a goldfish might): an image of a red bicycle. An image of a trumpet. A blonde girl. A traffic light. Another blue cat. Remember where the first cat is. Flip it. They match. Remove the cats. Flip another: a rose. Flip the original rose: an image of a trumpet appears.

"But I thought—"

"Memory has nothing to do with thinking."

If you think too much, you lose at Memory. If you describe a face from memory, your memory of the face begins to fade. This is scientific fact. The more you describe an image from memory, the more the memory disappears. Write down what an old friend looked like, and when you're through scribbling out how his nose was slightly broken, causing the bridge to turn sharply just below his eyes, his face recedes further into the darkness of soon-to-be-forgotten memories. Describe the blonde girl on the card: yellow pigtails with red hair ties, blue eyes, two dots to give the impression of a nose; she was smiling. Closed mouth? Hint of neck without a body.

Is that the same girl? As the first? Don't think about what she looks like. You'll lose it.

Your father had a scar on his chin. On the left side of his chin. Just a crevasse where something had sliced into him.

Flip a card: at the Weymouth tennis club: Dad removes his gold wedding ring and Ironman watch, threading the ring onto the band and clasping the watch back together. He slides the valuables into the zippered compartment of his gray, vinyl racquet bag and picks up the Prince Thunderstick, a doublewide tennis racquet. Flip another card: on the Meadow View tennis court: your brother stands at the baseline and throws his Prince Response like a Frisbee at the metal pole of the cage. The racquet cracks and collapses under the pressure of the strings. Flip another card: on the Big Sur, Mom says, "Look at the cliff. Oh my god," and laughs while: your brother sings "Free Falling." Flip another card: on campus, senior year, after school: you are sitting in a teacher's office asking her to help edit a short story you wrote on the side. Flip another card: Dad removing his wedding ring and Ironman watch, sliding them into the zippered compartment of his gray racquet bag. Remember where the original is. Don't think about it. If they are identical, remove them from the lot.

Just remember. Just flip the original. Flip the card: you, sitting in the teacher's office with the short story.

"But I thought—"

MONDAY AFTERNOON

My printer is spraying out papers and notes like a snow blower. I am grabbing at the flakes, eyes desperate, scanning. I toss the articles, grab new ones, search for a thread, a through-line, a center to this story, a point to make, this tale's grounding, its purpose, any clue.

If I am to speak at this bereavement group meeting in a room full of sad little high school and middle school kids, my story's got to be tight, straight. I am blazing through articles that I remember having something to do with loss, coping, grieving. I print synopses of famous memoirs of death. Old psych lectures from college about death, fear, loneliness. I am hunting for the story to tell, a concise, clean, clear, calm, cool mini-lecture to give these kids—a little speech that will seem improvised but will draw from sources, research, an illusion of my years studying the subject of loss, a representation of years of thinking deeply, coming to generous and helpful conclusions. I scramble to prepare for this new class tomorrow night, now that I am to be the teacher.

While driving from Saratoga Springs to Boston, on NPR came a snippet about a group of scientists who had tested the validity of the grief process. I knew the grief process, had heard it before, seen people in movies tell other people in movies that they are in the 'denial' stage and eventually they would arrive at the 'acceptance' stage. There was a proper way to go about being fucked up after a loss. Do it in proper order.

I print out the scientists' article and race through it. These geniuses had discovered that the grief process that we all know and love is actually wrong, worse than backwards! First of all, they say, the naming and ordering of the stages was simply made up. Fiction! These widely accepted stages and labels were never empirically experimented and were falsely, thusly categorized. No! Some dude just said all this shit and it stuck. What's more, the scientists of this article point out that for someone who has experienced loss and is trying to deal with it, to hear about the *proper* grief process compounds and hurts the healing journey. Because! No one is going to do it right.

No shit!

They are right!

I never methodically followed the grief process, and so thought I wasn't doing it correctly. Now, these scientists were telling me that I was doing it correctly no matter how I did it. Thank God!

This would make it into my mini lecture.

I read over stories of mine in which a character deals with death. Scan for good lines, something quotable, something grandiose and radio-friendly that I had coined, some creed to live and lose by. But I haven't written that yet.

I plan to mention my stories, how I've dealt through my private relationship with storytelling. Storytelling could be analogous to therapy sessions or painting or bringing a gun to school. *Whatever works for you as long as you think about the loss* is what I'm after in this vein.

I make up an outline to follow:

Introduction:
- "Hi, I'm Mark, and I first would like to say how brave I think all of you are for participating in this bereavement group. I never attended anything like this when I lost my father, my junior year of high school, and I think it is very mature to participate. So, I just want to say that to you, first off."
- Address them, compliment them right off the bat.
- Tell sketch of how Dad died and the days that followed.
- Explain how this affected you in your senior year of high school.

With Hope:
   • Along the way, someone will have a question, or say, "I know that feeling," and you can start to incorporate their voices, get everyone talking.

Multimedia:
   • Hand out this scientific article about the grief process.
   • Explain how it helped you to discover that you were normal.
   • Everyone wants to feel normal.
   • The worst thing for a high school or middle school kid is to be singled out for being different in some way, and having a dead dad is a sign on your back.
   • Teach them that they are normal.

Anecdote:
   • Tell an anecdote about a time that is counter-intuitive to how you thought you should be feeling after the loss.
   • How you thought that his grave would become this holy spot that you would visit every week and a place where you would continue to share your life with your father in some spiritual way, but that now when you go there, you feel nothing spiritual.
   • Tell of how you rarely go now. And how that is ok, too.
        - I am sure you will hear similar things from others, and they would all be scared to admit it, but if you admit it first, everyone will feel free to mention the same things.

Close it out:
   • Ask them questions.
        - Be funny, too.
        - Remember to be light at times.
        - *Life goes on* will be the unspoken lesson in a small joke.
        - Not everything has to be heavy.
        - You can laugh about times with your dad, too.

These kids will ride home with their parents and begin to talk, will report to their mothers something you said and how it made them think such and such a thing. Their lives will open up, and they will begin to heal. You can do this. If you stay focused. Be prepared. Be concise and human. Follow the plan. Stick to the outline. Do it in proper order.

GRAVE VISITS

[TEN YEARS AFTER]

On the tenth anniversary of his father's passing, Micah and his mother visited the gravesite with flowers.

"Ten years," his mom said. Micah put an arm around her shoulder. "His middle name wasn't Lee, you know," she said.

"I know," said Micah, and the two smiled. Strolled away.

JUNK MAIL

[SOME BEFORE, SOME AFTER,
SOME CONTEMPORARY]

There are things I am leaving out.

Does it matter that while I was in Iowa, visiting a friend at the writing school there, I, for reasons that completely eluded me then and continue to today, researched the meaning and origin of ZIP codes and discovered that it stands for Zone Improvement Plan, and that the very first Zone Improvement Plan code in the United States is for the town where my father grew up? Does this have meaning?

Is there any value in describing what it was like for my brother to walk the streets of San Francisco late at night, after hearing from his mother that his father had died? That he stumbled through traffic and nearly died himself? Would it be worthwhile at all to talk about how he had to sit on a plane for hours just to arrive home to see his fatherless brother and husbandless mother? How the ticket price for that flight was astronomical and how we actually discussed how much of a rip off it was?

Or how about how my mother says that her dog sometimes perks up and stares off, sensing something, and she believes it is the ghost of my father walking around the house? Is there a story in that?

What of the last interaction I had with my father? We argued about how to set up a VHS player. How about that? Is there anything to that? Where should that go?

I have left out important scenes with girlfriends. Moments in which my father's death came up. When I got so angry and jealous that they had their dads still. The times when I hung out with these girls' fathers, men who could have been nice and fatherly to me, who could have been inquisitive and caring, but who never were. How I loathed their family dynamics and wished for a girl who had lost her mom, or dad, or a brother, or a sister, or a close friend, or something other than a pet to feel connected to these girls. How sometimes I wished for a death in their families while with them, not to punish, but to not feel alone.

I have an image of my brother mowing the lawn with headphones on, which Dad had done two weeks previous to his dying. Do I try to enter my brother's head and push that mower and relate something meaningful about stepping into the shoes that he didn't think he'd have to? Should I talk about how much I love my brother and how I see that he has sacrificed? Do I write about how the only thing that can make me cry, really, is thinking of my mother alone in her house?

What about the shirts I wear that were my father's? How about the time I mistakenly put in a blank VHS tape only to see my father on a home movie? What that moment was like? Maybe the scene where my friend taught me how he shaves and how neither of us acknowledged how this was a scene meant for a father and son? Is there something to the fact that my dad taught me to tie a shoelace with two loops, and that's how I did it for a long time when everyone else was using one loop and how, at some point, in private, I switched to one loop?

These are all probably meaningless. These things left out. But I just can't stop wondering if examining these will unlock it, will let me go. I can't stop hoping that they'll work, that one of these scenes, stories, moments, details will be my last on the subject.

There was a man, an image, a life, and it was whole. Then it exploded, sending fragments to every corner of the world, every corner of my mind. If I can put it back together, maybe it will be whole again. But they are unnumbered, and they come together to form a new picture. Complete but never whole. There is a new order. Or the order itself has exploded, popped.

SWING SET UPKEEP

[THREE YEARS AFTER]

"Where's Daniel?" Mo asks his mother. His older brother is staying at home for the weekend, but he's nowhere in the house.

"He mentioned fixing something? Outside? I think he's doing yard work?"

Mo fills a coffee mug with a Boston Celtics logo on it and ventures outside in his pajama pants and bare feet to hunt his older brother.

Mo discovers Daniel in the side yard, holding an ancient axe with a blue handle. He's got the axe on his shoulder, and he's sizing up the dilapidated swing set. The swing set was an entire land of adventure and fun in their youth. Now, the swings have broken off, the slide's hanging on by maybe one screw, the four wooden supports that come out of the ground and hold the structure up are termite food. The monkey bars that stretch across from one side to the other are in various stages of presentness. It's a giant splinter.

Daniel's back is to Mo and he may not know that Mo is watching him. But Mo does watch, sipping coffee, head slightly cocked. Daniel is contemplating the swing set. He walks to one side, shakes the swing set, sees where it is loose, vulnerable. He readjusts the slide to give it more stability. He goes back to the front of the giant splinter and contemplates it some more.

Mo sips his coffee and squints up at the bright blue sky and nourishing warmth of the July sun. A bee buzzing by his ear. The smell of freshly cut grass. Mo's on summer vacation from college. Daniel is on his weekend vacation. Mo returns his gaze to his brother.

Daniel approaches the swing set cautiously, grabs hold of a monkey bar and shakes, examining the structure's constitution. He pulls on a chain that once held a swing. He steps back, regarding the whole play area, lifts the axe off his shoulder, raises it above his head, lunges forward, and splits the swing set in half, sending the bridge of monkey bars down in a loud creaking and snapping crash, cutting the thing in half. Daniel puts the axe on his shoulder, approaches the first support beam, stretching up from the ground. He bends down to assess the damage done by bugs and winters. He runs his finger along the base. Then Daniel stands up, squares himself to the support beam, positions himself as if waiting for a fastball and swings away at the support. Wood and metal burst into the air. He inspects the slide again, then steps back, holds the axe like a five iron, hits a drive that destroys the slide's last working hinge with a satisfying boom. The slide spins to the ground in a fury of dust and splinters, crashing down. Daniel measures and slaps an axe forehand winner that smashes out the second support beam. He blasts a topspin axe backhand to the deuce court that cuts the third support clear in half, collapsing the structure on itself, crumbling down. Daniel squares himself to the final supporting wood beam, pulls his toe back behind the invisible baseline tosses an invisible grenade into the air, reels back, springs upward, and hits an ace that blows apart the last support, buckling the whole swing set into a pile of dust and wood and metal. He leans over the mess of wood, the beams and rungs. He hacks away at it until it is small enough to carry away in his arms, trip by trip, into the forest. He heaves it all out of sight for good.

Mo goes in for a coffee refill and knows to not offer his help.

WHAT MORRIS IS PLANNING TO DO TOMORROW

[UNFORESEEABLE FUTURE]

Morris is making a plan for tomorrow. He will buy three new canisters of PENN tennis balls, pop them open, sniff the chemical green fuzz, and restring his dad's racquet. He will go to the Pequot Side court, where his dad taught him how to play. The court with cracks so deep he can't see down to their bottoms, long winding cracks like rivers viewed from a parachute; the court with more than grass growing up through its hardtop, the court with hay reaching up around the net. And if no one is there, Morris will practice his serve until his arm's about to fall off. He will get tired, sweaty, hot, and when he's almost delirious from serving, changing sides, collecting the balls, and serving and serving, he'll drive over to his dad's grave, just five minutes down Washington Street. He will have no expectations about what he'll feel when he's sitting on the manicured grass in front of the grave, touching the plaque with the incorrect name on it. With hope, he will be too exhausted to have any thoughts in his head: the wonderful thing about overexertion. If he passes out on the grass, he'll sleep. If he gets hungry, he'll leave and eat. But he won't write about any of it. He will refuse to, tomorrow. Maybe he'll tell someone, though. But he knows some things aren't for the page. That's all. He is not excited. It feels like obligation. Like a romantic obligation. And he wants the romance to end.

CRITIQUE

We say we really loved this piece. The details. The setting is beautiful. The dialog is spot on. We say this rang true. We say this is a universal concrete. We say that the ending was shocking but inevitable. The scene came to life with sensory details. We say great line. We say it was paced perfectly. We ask where did you come up with this? We say we laughed out when. We cried. We say it has energy. We say page-turner. We say it grabbed us. We say this captured it just so. We say you may have missed an opportunity here. With this character. We say the character needs more backstory. We say where's the conflict? We say wouldn't this character think this at that point? We say we want more interior monologue. We say we want to know how she feels. We say this took me out of the story. We say we couldn't figure out where we were in the story for a moment. We say typo. We say choppy. Fragment. Awkward. Reword. We say when thinking about a second draft you might. We say cut this. We say expand. We say one-dimensional. We say tonal shift. We say it's a problem of style here. We say it's the ending. Something's missing. We say cop out. We say slow starter. We say what's his goal? We say, are we supposed to care that she didn't achieve this? We ask what motivated that? We say we liked the font. We say this word doesn't mean what it is implied to mean there. We say vary sentence structure. We say watch the tense shifts. We say it's too long. Too short. We say the punch line didn't work for us. We say we've seen it before. We say you pulled this off the shelf. We say stock. Cliché. Too easy. Rehashed. Trite. We say what if you put it in present tense? Switched it to second person? What about fourth future perfect continuous conditional? We say rip off. We say copy. We say published. We say rejected. We say winner. We say editor. We say agent. We say sales. We say book deal. We say foreign rights. We say out of print. We say public domain. We say read this! We say we hated it. We say adaptation. We say doesn't live up. We say bad translation. We say any recommendations? We say what if you? We say we make the same mistake all the time. We say good dialog comes from not answering. We say mixed metaphor. We say this feels like memoir. Like fictional. We say have you ever read so and so? We say that we are simply biased when it comes to. We say filmic. Unreal. Unbelievable. Genre. We say we want to be entertained. We say we want more depth. We say we don't want a moral. We say we want to learn something. We say you wrote yourself into the story. We say start here. We say that so and so says this. We say plot point. We say twist. We say saw it coming. We say experimental. Traditional. Absurd. Fabulist. Magical realism. Modernist. Postmodernist. Post-neo. Post-characterist. Post-storyist. We say break through. We say mind blowing. We say slipstream. New wave. We say it's all been done before. We say there's no accounting for. We say but what do we know? We say that's just our opinion. We say thanks for the read. We say thanks for reading.

THE PURPOSE OF FICTION

[EIGHT YEARS AFTER]

Mattie had read about this Professor, heard *things*. The Professor was, according to a former student and now critically acclaimed author, and one of Mattie's favorites: a man on autopilot who should not be teaching anymore. The Professor was, according to former students who were either not yet or never going to be critically acclaimed authors: only interested in the type of fiction he himself writes. The Professor was, according to Garewood: an old friend, fiercely intelligent, beware of him. Garewood went on to say that 'something went wrong with him,' him being the Professor in question. That Garewood used to be friends with the Professor, and Garewood was Mattie's idol, and that they had a complicated relationship that revolved around fiction, and then the relationship took a bad turn, and something about the Professor 'went wrong'—this was all too much amazing. Who was this guy, and what was he going to do for Mattie? Mattie's writing? What kind of reverse mirror, negative imprint of Garewood would this man be? Garewood already being a father figure, and this Professor having read Garewood's stories when he was Mattie's age, seeing the early pieces of Garewood's eventually-Pulitzer-winning stuff—this was special and exciting. Mattie was anxious to meet him, to tell him of his friendship/mentorship with Garewood, to become special to this Professor, to have an in. An in to somewhere mysterious. A new potential father? Could Mattie amass several?

Mattie's mental projection of the Professor was almost spot on: inches over six feet, solid, full head of white hair, a beard, casually dressed, with a booming voice that also had a slight rasp. What to make of picturing someone almost perfectly? Does one take this as a sign? A sign that other projections should be equally prophetic? Mattie's imagining of their budding mentorship? Could it be?

In the first workshop, the Professor distributed a handout with recommended readings. On the list? None other than Garewood's first book. A book that was unknown to nearly all in the workshop, a type of obscure thing. Even through their estrangement, spanning some twenty years, the Professor kept a place on his list for Garewood. Garewood had never mentioned the Professor or his writings before Mattie told him where he was to attend graduate school. And even then, Garewood hesitated. He leaned back, squinted, said the name of the Professor. Said, 'I knew him.' An awkward and deliberate use of the past tense. Garewood did not know him now.

Mattie was delighted to see the book on the list, felt that this was the beginning of a new chapter, a new learning experience, that maybe he would evolve from what Garewood taught him, evolve into some hybrid of these two great, intelligent men. Each of them had, in distinct ways, success and praise. Now, would they together, in this perfect alignment of stars, create Mattie, the writer? The final chapter of this battle. And Mattie did frame it as a battle: Garewood, the dreamer. The Professor, the strict realist. A literary philosophy battle. Mattie would emerge from both, in the middle, never settling the thing.

After the first workshop of Mattie's story, which went well, the two met in the Professor's office to discuss the piece.

"Send it to the *New Yorker*," the Professor said. Immediately, the Professor endeared himself to Mattie. He was already switching sides at this never-before-heard-of praise. "They'll never accept it," the Professor continued. "But they might. It's perfect!" Mattie was in love.

"You know, I studied with Garewood in college."

"Oh, Garewood. Wow! We were friends."

"I know. He told me to say hi for him." Did he?

"Do tell him I say hi as well. I'd love to see him again." Mattie wondered if Garewood would not want the same. What was so bad about this Professor? What had gone wrong with him? He loved Mattie's work. Garewood was worried the Professor would change Mattie's aims. So far, he was perfectly encouraging. What the heck?

Mattie rode high on the *New Yorker* comment, and he did in fact send it over their way. It was not accepted. But that proved nothing.

The Professor mentioned playing basketball to the class. It was a side note. He loved basketball and wanted everyone to join in the games he played, if they all wanted.

Basketball!

What more could one ask for!? A doting professor who also played ball? This was it. This story was unfolding ideally.

It turned out that the Professor and Mattie were the only ones to show when it came time to play. Garewood played Ping-Pong; The Professor, basketball. Mattie and his father enjoyed both activities, but neither activity was tennis. The two played one-on-one, the way Mattie and his dad used to. A taller, broader, older man playing a post-up game against the thinness of Mattie, who mostly enjoyed dribbling. But Mattie couldn't perform the way he would have liked, because the Professor was older and slower and maybe a step away from a broken hip, and Mattie's experience was on the courts of Boston, against showoffs, in which the game was about who could break whose ankles and drain a jumper. Mattie crossed up the Professor once, saw how he stumbled, got too nervous to ever try it again. And so, the post-up game prevailed.

In-game, checking the ball: "What do you think of Garewood's stories?"

"I can't read them." Can't read them? "They are all the same. It's all the same all the time. One after another. I can't read it anymore. I know exactly what's coming."

Mattie took personal offense to this. The Professor drove hard to the hoop. The Professor's heavy high top squashed Mattie's toe on the way to a layup. The toe broke. He heard and felt the snap. Mattie knew it, but he kept playing, unable to show a weakness after such a comment. Shock plus pride kept his feet moving.

Afterwards, Mattie went to the emergency room where it was, indeed, declared broken and a splint was applied to the toe, doing very little for the pain of walking. He removed it the following morning when struggling with a sock.

The second story of Mattie's up for workshop was less well received by the class and the Professor. The story tested the dream water, leaned toward Garewood's side of the game. Distrusting of strict realism.

In the Professor's office:

"Fiction is different than other art forms. There is a reason why fiction exists and movies exist. Why poetry exists. Why sculpture exists. Why all these things exist. They serve purposes that the others don't satisfy. Fiction tells us how characters feel. In a movie, you can't be in a character's head. You have to read their faces. In stories, you can be told a character's thoughts, feelings, desires, goals, everything. How does your character feel? Tell us how he feels!"

Then Mattie was at a loss. This Professor who had been built up so much as a strict shouldn't-be-teaching-anymore type guy, who loved Mattie's first story and played basketball and was interesting to talk to if argumentative, was slowly fading away. The Professor was transforming into an enemy. His height turned menacing; his big smiles turned sharp; his comments manipulative.

Mattie's final story for class was a dream. It was a straight dream. Slipping around. Playing with imagery, completely disregarding *telling* how characters felt. It was about death. It was a statement. And this story made Mattie an enemy of the Professor.

The story's main character has suffered the loss of a loved one. This beloved person had drowned, and the main character, called simply The Man, experiences this in the final scene:

Excerpt: "The Man"

The Man clicked off his only lamp, there next to him. The light of the moon streamed into his apartment through the slats in the blinds. He lit a cigarette and exhaled in a long straight line, watching as the smoke dusted for and revealed the path of white moonlight pouring through the slats in the blinds in hard white bars. He exhaled again and illuminated the path of moonlight from the window all the way down to the floor before him. The smoke dissipated, and he snuffed out the cigarette. Ten channels of white light lay between him and the photo. He crawled forward to examine the light on the floor— perfect straight lines of white with perfect straight lines of black in between. Hard and defined. Ten moonlight bars.

He tapped at the channels, dabbed at them. His fingertips felt wet, and he examined them. A black inky substance coated his hand. He held his hand to the moonlight. The black liquid dripped from his fingertips. He did not understand. He returned to the bars of white moonlight on his floor, studied them closely. He swiped at the channels again—they were wet. And he remembered the path of white light, the path of black sky in between. It was not the white light that streamed through the slats in the blinds. It was the night. The black night poured down onto his hardwood floor. He pushed at the bars of night on his floor, playing curiously with the liquid sky. In the course of splashing his floor, the picture frame fell over with the noise of a water droplet into the sink. He scraped furiously over the black channels, erasing the white bars, spilling the puddles of night sky over the white lines. He sloshed the black liquid over the whiteness until his entire floor was blackness—all liquid night without a drop of moonlight.

A moment passed. The Man stood, unlatched the window, pushed it up, and a rush of black sky spilled into his new place.

In the darkness, The Man heard his apartment squeaking, swelling, snapping. The black liquid filled his room, gently lifting up the boxes, the lamp, the coffee table, the sofa—vague dark shadows floated, rose through the black living space. The shapes drifted to all corners of his place, then sailed out beyond the edges of the room, and the black liquid spread infinitely. Soon, The Man felt an odd buoyancy and was raised from the floor, floating, wading in the rising blackness, engulfed by the night sky. The liquid rose and covered his eyes, his head. He held his breath in the warm spreading black sea, and then took a long, deep breath, sucking in night sky, and found he could breathe just fine. The Man swam about, opening his eyes wide to scan for his things, his room, his new place, but quickly he could no longer tell which way was up, which down, and he spun lazily in the blackness, rising and falling, turning and turning, drifting away. Was this what it was like for his Lena? Was it a comfort? Was it disturbing? He could not yet tell, but he accepted it. He would stay here for a time. He pulled off his blazer, spun about, removing his shoes and socks, floating, undressing. He stretched and twisted. He struggled for a moment to find where to go, how to move in this new place. He looked to the moon, a perfect circle, a circular cutout in the black ceiling of the universe, promising a white room on the other side. He swam up and up, fixing his eyes on the white room on the other side. Suddenly, he felt a rush of current and was borne away to the beaches of quiet, black islands.

He drowns in ink. It takes him away. Get it?

In the meeting:

"I don't know what to make of this at all. I have no access to how your character feels. It's fiction. So. How does this character feel?"

Mattie thought about this. Thought about the purpose of fiction. Thought about what makes a story a story and not something else, like the Professor had said. Thought about Garewood's stories and how he loved them. He looked at this Professor.

And he said: "I have no idea how I feel. That's why I write. Why I write these things instead of… Instead of."

TUESDAY MORNING

At the copy store, the copying machine's asking for more paper. I get the guy, feel as though I'm bothering him. I don't have much time, I think all the time. The scientists' article, one of my stories, an excerpt from a loss memoir, and a sheet with my contact info are all laid out on the counter next to the machine. When the guy's finished reloading the paper, I stick the article in the shoot and ponder how many copies to make. Fifteen? What do fifteen kids look like? In a community center or church basement or wherever this is? I see a classroom of fifteen kids in rows. Maybe one of mine. One diligent girl up front with her papers in order, ready for the day's lesson, with her questions and answers prepared, absorbing herself in this studiousness to avoid what? I see the bigger boy on the far right, nearer to the wall of windows, every once in a while looking out one of them. He has lost his backpack but is not a slacker; he hasn't got his shit together. Thirteen more in rows. This is a special class, an involuntary elective. Coping. I see the kid I'm supposed to talk to, who isn't doing well. He's in the back. He's tall, thin as anything, with hair flopping in front of his face. He has no backpack either, but he isn't concerned about this. He leans forward on his desk, places his chin on the backs of his folded hands. He is smiling a little. What's in his pocket? What's in his face? Can I hand this kid a neat packet? Can I make him academic about his dad dying? *That smile.*

This is completely useless, this whole idea. This can't be taught, only learned.

I throw the stack of handouts in the recycling bin and charge out into the wind.

"HE SUGGESTED I BURN THE MOTHER."

[NINE YEARS AFTER]

Morgan's first real teaching gig was at the writing school in the desert. The undergrad honors students needed an instructor for their Intro to Fiction course, and Morgan got the call.

Looking down the class roster, he saw the name Sam Malone. "You kidding me?" he said out loud to no one in his hot little adobe hut. "The effing bartender from *Cheers*? Yes!"

But Sam Malone ordered the class to call him Strike, maybe because of this connection to pop culture. Skinny as anything. Tattoos. Black hair flopping in front of his face. Headphones in ears until class began and headphones in ears right after the bell. There was no bell.

"I have a problem," Rebecca, one of the more dedicated and promising students began in Morgan's office during a one on one meeting. "I got a comment on my story that really bothered me."

"You have to tell me," Morgan said, and he felt himself acting responsible, serious all of a sudden. She didn't have to tell him.

"I feel weird, because I don't want to start a witch hunt with the Virginia Tech shootings and—"

"Rebecca, you have to tell me." People had been shot dead by a VT student only days before.

"One of the students just made a suggestion that felt really aggressive."

"What did this student write on your story?"

"He suggested I burn the mother."

Strike's stories were sick. They were about vicious murder, blood, rape, torture, fire, monsters preying on the innocent. Usually small innocent girls. Usually disemboweling. Which is not cool. But it is only one fecta of the tri needed to nail down someone as *psycho.*

"Strike?" Morgan ventured. Who else?

"Yes." Rebecca obviously felt like a narc, felt like a prissy little thing. This is what keeps us from doing anything. The fear of not also being seen as bad, as rebellious. Scared to be cautious and thoughtful.

"Do you have his comments with you?"

"Yes." She handed Morgan the comments. He read them while she waited. Before Morgan finished, eyes still cast down to the paper, she added: "I don't feel safe in class. That's why I sit closest to the door all the time now."

"I'll take care of this."

"I don't want to start a witch hunt."

What Rebecca left out was that Strike also wanted the mother character to rape her son in the story. Then the son character to burn his mother. The story was about a tennis tournament.

The desert's always bright. Always blue. The atmosphere did not align with the darkness of the situation. It made Morgan feel like an idiot. The nice days. These things happen in the dark, in the cold. It's difficult to maintain an air of seriousness and darkness when the flat blue sky and hazy sun won't quit saying, "Well isn't this nice?"

"I have a problem," Morgan told the senior faculty advisor, a young and cool guy in the Creative Writing department, an awesome short story writer. Morgan looked up to him.

"Bring it by my office."

Situation brought.

"I'll take care of this," he said. Morgan felt in good, cool hands.

"We have a problem," the senior faculty advisor and Morgan said to the dean of student affairs.

Problem presented.

"I'll take care of this," she said and pointed to an aluminum baseball bat in the corner of her office. "You see that? That's no joke."

Three emails from female students informed Morgan that they were no longer going to attend class.

This is his first fucking teaching gig? Teaching, the only thing Morgan ever wanted to do with his life. Life saying, "Care to rethink?"

Morgan got Strike into a meeting at his office, then sprung it on him that they were going to walk over to another office and have a talk with the senior faculty advisor. They walked across campus. Strike scraped his feet, scratching the concrete loudly, slow as hell three paces behind Morgan. Morgan kept looking back. Checking. Expecting to see he didn't know what.

The meeting was a disaster. The senior faculty advisor had told Morgan that he was anxious to have the meting, that he couldn't wait to have this fucking psycho in his office and set him straight. If the little fucking asshole didn't talk, if he appeared to be a fucking psycho, the senior faculty advisor was going to fucking get him the hell away from campus. The senior faculty advisor had demons of his own, Morgan was sure, and wanted to unleash them.

Strike said about three words. Morgan said zero. The senior faculty advisor at one point said this: "I love brutal, gory fiction. You know," he chuckled, lost, scared. "One of my favorite books is the most violent vicious thing." Then, the senior faculty advisor grabbed the world's most violent book and handed it to Strike. "Here," he insisted. "Take it."

Strike left the meeting, a free man-psycho.

The senior faculty advisor and Morgan sat in silence for a while in his office. Morgan wanted to say, *what the fuck was that all about? You nearly encouraged more psycho shit! You got all red in the face and let him walk, now I have to go to class with scared students and a little fucker! I needed you to be cool!*

"He's definitely psycho," said the senior faculty advisor, voice now lowered, serious. "I don't know what just happened."

It occurred to Morgan that this whole thing could be reframed: Strike could have serious problems, he could be crying for help, you know. Morgan could simply ask him if he was all right, be a sympathetic character in Strike's life. Make a difference. He was sure a kid looking the way Strike looks doesn't get much good attention, sympathy. Then, while editing a story in the morning, sipping coffee, in his hot little adobe hut, listening to NPR on the portable RadioShack radio, Morgan heard that one of the Virginia Tech murderer's Creative Writing professors had believed that the future murderer just needed sympathy. She felt she could help save him. Make a difference.

Meaning of story immediately lost. Coffee instantly cold. Confidence speeding away into the desert. Morgan's delusions of saviordom just fell straight off a cliff.

Strike's final story was up for workshop in the last class of the semester. A jaunty piece of prose about a home invasion that leads to the hanging and quartering of an innocent family.

The senior faculty advisor, maybe in need of redemption after his emasculation in the botched disciplinary meeting, decided to attend the class, claiming to be eager to tackle the little fucker if he reached toward his backpack for a gun or something. "I'll just fucking take him out," he cheered.

Morgan emailed all the girls who had ceased to attend class, informing them that they would be accompanied by a senior faculty advisor and that armed security guards would be right outside the door—a precaution the dean wanted them to have. It would be safe, he told the long-absent girls. Please attend the last meeting.

Morgan arrived at the senior faculty advisor's office before class, gave him a copy of Strike's story up for workshop. They waited for the clock to hit eleven. It finally did. The senior faculty advisor cracked his knuckles and the two exited the safety of his high bunker.

Little Strike Malone never reached for his backpack, didn't take the opportunity to tell the class anything psychotic, didn't really do anything but doodle on his own story during the final meeting.

The senior faculty advisor certainly took the opportunity to talk wild and nervous, though. He discussed the story with the workshop, again going all red in the face, higher in the voice. At one point he said this: "you know, violence is part of life. Some of this is great." He blew it again. The no bell rang, and it was all almost over.

Morgan did have a final one-on-one meeting with Strike. He gave him suggestions for revision, ways to maybe reveal backstory on the deranged serial killer in the story, and other bullshit to fill the time. But just before everything was over and done with and history and behind them, Morgan asked him, point blank: "What the fuck?"

Strike leaned forward. He flashed a shit-eating smile. And he told Morgan the fuck.

TUESDAY MORNING

"I'm out"

"What do you mean you're out?"

"I mean, you lied to me, and I'm not prepared to do this, and I don't think I can do this, and I don't even agree with the whole enterprise."

"Mark!"

"I'm sorry. But what about me? Have you considered whether I'd have trouble with this?"

"..."

"Have you?"

"..."

"I just don't want to go and talk with these kids. I have no idea what to tell them. I haven't reached some serene place in this whole thing either, and I'm no expert."

"..."

"I am still wondering if I have done anything."

"..."

"I have never done anything like this before, and for the first time that I am to be doing it, I'd like to know a little more than twenty-four hours in advance. To think about it."

"..."

"So. Fuck it. I'm out."

"I don't really want to go either."

"What?"

"I don't really want to do this either."

"..."

"I could just say that I'm not feeling well."

"Good."

" … "

"Maybe another time."

" … "

MEETING

[SEVEN YEARS AFTER]

"I want to first say to all of you how great it is that you've come here to participate in this endeavor," Mitchell said first to the new faces seated before him. The small graduate student-run literary magazine's office was a hundred-year-old adobe in Tucson, with hundred-year-old couches, with fluff exploding from cushions, and hundred-year-old bookcases, bowing under the weight of twenty-five years worth of back issues. Some of the new faces were attached to bodies that sat in desk chairs and folding chairs brought out of closets for the meeting. Some of the new bodies were seated cross-legged on the floor, legs tucked under butts on couch cushions. Some new faces were being stuffed with slices of pizza and red plastic cups of Coke and Pepsi, all of which were provided by the meeting's powers that be. The unconditioned air rising in temperature, the floors and walls covered with people, and everywhere hot pizza boxes. "I want to say that we have a great opportunity, a chance to really do something good with our time here. And we will need to rely on one another over the course of this challenge." What the hell was he saying? Who talks like this?

Mitchell had hastily planned (imagined is more accurate) the little speech, didn't get much past the opening lines, hoping that adrenaline and the surroundings would propel the rest of the words. He felt immediately ill-equipped: he should have prepared a plan of action, but he thought it would sound insincere to be so prepared and rehearsed. He thought that everyone would think him a nerd or no-fun leader, or worse, a fraud. He wanted all the new faces to view him as a mostly-fun leader, leaderly enough to not have to prepare everything down to the finest details, able to wing it with confidence. So, he was winging it. Winging it like everything else he does.

"How's the pizza?" he asked of the new faces, trying to think up something great to say while the crowd responded to the question and hopefully decided that he was funny and mostly fun.

"Good!" shouted a mouth full of pepperoni.

"Well, there's more pizza where that pizza came from, if we accomplish our goals!" Mitchell proclaimed in a half joking, half *am-I-serious?* tone. "Much more pizza and Pepsi!" At this point, he figured that everyone deduced they could get away with just about anything with a leader like him at the helm. So, he shifted gears, became serious, confused everyone. "But there will be no pizza, if we slack off."

"Awww," boomed the crowd of new faces.

"I'm sorry," Mitchell said. "This is serious stuff." Mitchell looked around the room, searching for a prop, something to talk about. Metal bookshelves with hundreds of volumes of literary magazines. Hot black sky out the window. What were the goals? What is so serious about this? "We have a great opportunity," he repeated, using the oral storytelling tradition of repetition to buy time and think up the next part of the story. "This year, we will increase circulation, promote the magazine at book fairs, with readings, at the conference in Atlanta. We will make this magazine a household name!" Vague but somewhat truthful of the hopes he had for the literary journal. "As the Editor," he embarked. "I am here to make sure everything behind the scenes gets done and support all of you to contract the best fiction, nonfiction, poetry, interviews, and book reviews possible, which reminds me. Book reviews are a new pursuit for the journal: we will have book reviews for the first time. After all, we are called a 'Review,' so it should, technically, have reviews in it. And, this is an opportunity for some of you to review a book and have your review published in the Review. So start thinking now of books

you'd like to review, propose them, and you may write one... Yes?
You in the back?"

"Where's the bathroom?'

"Yes, the bathroom... A great question, and I'm glad you asked. The
bathroom, all of you take note, is in the adjacent room. There are two
doors in the adjacent room, and the door farthest to the back of the
room is the door to the bathroom... Any other questions?"

There were no other questions. Everyone already knew the score:
this was a grad school literary journal, and they all were to read
submissions of fiction, nonfiction, and poetry and decide whether or
not the pieces were worthy of publication. It was a straightforward
thing. These people didn't need a leader at all. Mitchell just wanted
to be needed. He ended his opening address and grabbed a slice of
pizza himself, disappearing into the bodies on the area rug, against
the wall, mingling, chatting out on the hot adobe porch. Everyone
picked up papers from stacks of slush and commenced reading,
judging, wielding new literary power, enjoying lines, hating lines.
Mitchell knew that he was spotted, that everyone had pegged him
properly as a man without much to impart, that he was essentially
in the same boat as everyone else. It's just that he had got on board
one year before them. So, this lent some sort of authority to his
presence. Something he was eager but unable to embody, it turned
out. He couldn't help these new faces, because he still needed so
much help himself.

Maybe, though, he thought: maybe it's enough to have all these
others along for the ride?

TUESDAY AFTERNOON

Once again I have no plans, nothing on the horizon, nothing to prepare for. An unstructured life, nowhere to be. Ever. So, I go to the laptop with a Miller, though it's just after noon, and open up Word, see what I have going on there.

I pull up a story at random, one of the many half-finished variety: one about a kid who begins receiving letters addressed to someone else at his new apartment in the desert. He tries to correct this at the post office. But the letters just keep coming, addressed to this person who is no longer living. In his apartment.

Excerpt: "Last Letters"

Charles Lin keeps getting mail at my place. And it's not like I just moved in. Bank statements at first, gas bills, the city shopper, his SI subscription (the first piece of mail I kept, thank you, Chuck), then packets from Tiffany and Co., a tiny box from *Guns and Ammo*. I wrote "Return to sender" on all of it. At first.

It's just that they kept coming—the same places, ignoring my returns, insisting that Charles Lin still lives in my house. Then letters, postcards. I sent them back. They would return to me. Over and over. The people, even those who seemed to know—handwritten address and all—kept sending, printing the address more clearly, bigger, no mistakes could be made. They knew Charles Lin lived in my apartment.

It had been exactly a month since I had last seen Andrea when a lipstick sealed envelope arrived for Charles Lin. And instead of adding it to the pile of envelopes that had "Return to Sender" stamped three times over them, I opened it. I said: there might be a reason I'm getting this stuff, this man's letters, statements, online purchases. Maybe I was Charles Lin in another life, but that was fluff. I didn't think big about it. I just, that day, said I need a little entertainment, and no one's going to know, and I'm entitled after all these attempts to properly return the items—I'm taking a look. That's all it was. At first.

A short thing. A love letter, to be sure, was the first thing I read. The lipstick. I knew it would be a good comedy or good romance letter. It turned out to have that mix of clichés and specificity about love that love letters, ones I've read, seen, used to, always seem to have. An example: "When you were inside me, Charles, I knew we were one." Now that's them having sex, and her, her name, by the way is Loraine (no last name (not even on the return address part of the upper left hand corner exterior of the envelopes, and sometimes just L mixed with x's and o's)) and Loraine is using a cliché—we were "one" like implying meant for each other, my other half, us joining together to form one person—an old idea. But she followed it up with this: "And when the sea gull shat on our beach towel, I knew it was a sign." That's specific. That's Loraine and Charles on the beach. There they are, thinking, Isn't this nice to relax? and maybe they smile at each other and Charles goes in for a dip, he gets knocked down by a wave and Loraine laughs, and they talk about how they need to pick up some wine for the party at Fred and Kathryn's that evening, but right then a sea gull shits on their towel. That's them. Not me. Not that *other half* shit—specific and cliché together. And it makes me feel like these people exist. That Charles Lin *is* alive and well and has this Loraine who likes him for him and they are funny together but also sentimental. A good story. I was entertained. I put the letter back into the envelope and placed it on my nightstand.

Loraine's letters arrived every Saturday. I would wake up, make coffee, check the clock, and wait for the postman, sometimes grabbing him as he placed the letters and other statements for Charles Lin into my mailbox. "I'll take those."

"Love sick, huh?"

"Huh?"

"I know when people are anticipating their lovers' notes. I'm the fucking postman for Christ's sake," said the mailman, who I later learned was named William. He had a theory about mail: when you get mail in this era of Internet and all that—when you get a letter from someone who has taken the time to put pen to paper, lick the envelope, address it, take it to the post office or drop box, mail, and then wait, they have patience, confidence that the parcel (his word) will arrive not instantly but in a few days—you've got someone who thinks about you day and night until that letter is read, and after the letter is read, the other person can stop thinking, just feel, feel good. I listened to his theory while shirtless in the street, holding Loraine's latest. I liked that this mailman, this William, had a theory about mail, because if he didn't, his job and existence would be less comforting, if he found out I wasn't who I was pretending to be. If he caught on to me, he would understand or something? His story about the goodness of letters was appreciated, at least, and noted. Definitely noted.

And things were great! I got updates on what Loraine was up to on the other side of the country. She had finally found a job! Finally. She had been griping about it and griping about it. But she decided to take a risk and pursue set design in the theater. I was happy. With her transition back east, she decided to switch careers, too.

I said, out loud, "good for you, Loraine," there in my apartment, shirtless on a Saturday afternoon. She has so much potential as a designer. She shouldn't be working in marketing anymore. She moved on, figured herself out. My outbursts, my exclamations at her choices started to become more regular, almost like we were talking, or I was a confessor—she saying that people in this industry just invest all of themselves in their work and lose touch with what matters most: friends, family, love (she meant Charles (and I caught the subtly)). I would nod my head, mutter hmmm, hmm, yup yup you're right. When you're right you're right. You know?

Eventually, the SI subscription evaporated. The online purchases dried up. The bank statements gobbled up by the void. All that remained, after a time, were Loraine's Saturday letters. Fine by me!

And I don't know why it didn't occur to me before, but after ten letters, she finally addressed the fact that I (Charles, really) hadn't responded. She wasn't angry or anything. She was whimsical, hopeful. Loraine wouldn't be angry with Charles Lin. They were inside each other and all that shit with the sea gull. When I read the line: "Charles? Charles, I wonder sometimes if you'll somehow respond…" I thought about why I hadn't written back. Obviously, Charles isn't getting this mail, but why hadn't I written? I could have signed it, Charles. I could have kept them connected, because there was no way of getting Charles his mail or convincing Loraine that he didn't live here anymore. I could have written. Something, anything, something like: "I'm busy with the awning business" (something I picked up from her letters), but my handwriting would give it away. I could type it.

And that's what I finally did, betraying William's theory on the power of handwriting, the time it takes, the personality inherent in the letter shapes. Beautiful man. All I said was that I was busy, but lived for her letters. That I thought about her all week and when I read her words, I smiled. It was the highlight of my week, as I spend it alone, alone, alone. The awning business is booming and all I do is sign contracts, stay up late at the office, come home and cook frozen meals. (I indulged, took some risks, put some of myself in it). That I rent movies and speak mostly with the rental girl clerks at the local store. I buy groceries and am continually unsure what is healthy, what is bad. That I think about letters a lot, but am too tired or too trite to write them. I would have written earlier but am loathsome in my uneventful ways. I have nothing to report but love for you Loraine. I am sorry, but it is all I have. That I eat cereal in the morning, staring at the wall, wondering when we could be together again.

I mailed my letter in the middle of the night, under cover of darkness. I waited another four days for her response.

When the letter didn't come, when I was standing there, waving to William, who just put his head down as he parked, I knew I was, for sure, a fool to write her. She knew it wasn't her Charles. Charles wouldn't have said all that shit about honestly considering a tattoo of a sea gull above his bellybutton, the center of him, where he was separated from one person only to be connected to another, to you, Loraine. I had been discovered and now was going to pay the price.

"Nothing today, Charles."

"Well, that happens right? I mean you guys don't sort it perfectly all the time. You guys fuck up right?"

"We're the Post Office, Chuck. We don't fuck up. All that's fucked up here is your lady. So, she sent it late, whatever. It will be here Monday. But I wouldn't count on it, Chucky boy. You got dumped."

"But I just opened myself up to her?"

"What?"

"I gave in. I told her that I loved her. Finally."

"The Post Office has a way of breaking hearts as well as keeping them intact. Plenty of parcels in the sea, right?"

"So, it will be here Monday?"

"What?" And William blew a snot rocket onto the pavement near my feet, sped off, wobbling.

The narrator dude realizes that the letters were to a dead man (probably after the reader realizes this, which is a big problem in this one). He writes another letter, and the reader has come to understand that this is a letter to free the woman of her pain. Or, if not completely free her, to give her something that will help her cope. The N is attempting to ease her pain with the letter. And the reader knows this before any words are written. Before anything becomes words. You already know that he is trying to do something about grief for someone else. You already know that he is to use his words, his ink to move forward in his life, help someone else move forward in hers. So, it doesn't matter what he writes. But I haven't written that part of the story yet. I can't tell you what he writes to the grieving Loraine.

The story's got that same formulaic structure that "Porcelain God" has—start off with the complicating symbol or issue (toilet left behind or, here, letters addressed to another person won't stop coming). Then expand from the problem to the focal character's inner issue (dead dad or, here, a hole in his heart over a girl he's left behind, which needs more developing). Then: so on, so forth, weaving them together. Both are about someone missing—Charles Lin being dead, the dad being dead, the girl being gone. It's always about being incomplete.

I finish reading over this piece. I glance at six other documents and rattle off what they're about before opening them: death, death, girl, loss, girl, death. I look at the first empty can of Miller on my desk. Look at the second half drunk can in my hand. Look at the stories. Look at what this particular story needs, think about how to finish it, what to say. Look at the time. One post meridian. The computer screen turns to psychedelic screen-saving spirals. A cold down draft that forecasts rain chills me from the skylight. The smell of a cigarette burning in an ashtray. Sweat on the can of Miller tickles my knuckle. I think that I should write that final benevolent letter to Loraine in the story.

I call my mom and tell her I'll be at her house by 5:30.

TENNIS

[TWO YEARS BEFORE]

The PENN cans popped. The wedding band and wristwatch clasped and thrown in the gray zippered racquet bag, placed under the bench. A few volleys backed and forthed. Then I take a real crack at one served up on a tee from my dad. Laser. Stays low and away.

"Whew!" my dad shouts. Really delighted. "You haven't lost anything!"

It's been a while since we've played. I think I had routine adolescent things to do, instead of great things.

"It never leaves me."

My dad's socks are white and crinkly-looking, halfway up his shin. My socks are tucked into my sneakers. My racquet is a loner from Nevada Bob's, where they let you demo racquets, where you can buy stringing machines for your father for Father's Day. The racquet I'm demoing, it's Boris Becker's. I love it. I fucking love it.

He serves. I slice a forehand and charge the net, but he can't get to it.

"That two-fisted forehand slice is unbelievable," he remarks.

"Really?"

"Whew!"

The weird thing about my game, which became not so weird after Monica Seles rose to prominence, is that I have a two-fisted forehand. This is uncommon. And, still, no man uses a two-fisted forehand in the ATP.

"I don't practice, and I'm better than you," I say. I'm joking until it's out of my mouth. I'm not better than my father at tennis. He is good, because he practices. He plays every week. He enters tournaments. He is fit. He runs. He was drafted for pro baseball. He has coached my basketball teams and Dave's baseball teams. My father is a fan of the game. He understands how to appreciate a shot, a training regimen. He is a player. A gamer. I am a snot. I have good athletic genes. Thanks to him. But I don't do anything. I barely show up. But it feels good to hit the ball. It feels right. It feels like biology freed. Nothing would please my dad more than for me to beat him. But I can't. I just can't. I haven't practiced.

We play.

My serve's all over the place. His is consistent. He calls balls in that I know I hit long. Still, I lose.

He wants to get root beer, offers to treat me to ice cream.

I forget if we got those snacks. I just wanted to win without trying, without putting in the time. Like everything else. Like writing. I just wanted to be gifted. At tennis. At art. At grieving. But it all takes practice.

ACES

[ON TELEVISION]

The most debilitating thing to do when performing a serve is to think about what you are doing. To become aware that your hips pull back slowly to draw your left leg at a forty-five degree slope down to the baseline, where your toe is a nanometer behind the white chalk; to think about your right elbow cutting perpendicular to your left arm as it tosses the ball; to understand that your ACL, MCL, and PCL, are slipping around your kneecap, coiling, building; to think about the height of the net and the impossibility of a ball passing over it with your reach without striking it at a nearly imperceptible cut, adding spin; to remember that you should watch the ball collide with the racquet before lowering your eyes to pick up on its landing inside the server's box; to think about following through so that your right hand taps the extra ball stored in your left pocket; to recall who it is that you are competing against.

To think about any of this is death to the serve.

You're supposed to go blank.

The same holds true for shooting a bucket, throwing and catching a pigskin, slapping a puck, hitting a homerun. You are ordered to stop thinking. And that's perfectly fine. As long as you've practiced. Your body knows better than your head, at this point, what to do. For once in your life: just go through the motions. Empty out and serve.

This is why, besides the irregularity of his playing in the past years, that Mark now sucks at serving. He can't stop thinking about it. Maybe if he practices his serve, like he's promised himself, soon, then he can just let go.

An ace, a good one, feels like nothing. It feels like you've come in contact with nothing. They say the same thing about throwing a knockout punch. Once you turn your brain on again, it might register as a mistake. Because your brain can't do this. When something's done properly, it's like you've done nothing at all. This is why Mark likes watching pro athletes so much. It's not that Goran Ivanesivich or Boris Becker or Patrick Rafter or Pete Sampras or Roger Federer were so finely tuned and smart, though they were. It's that, you can watch, right in front of your eyes, someone reaping the benefits of practice. Someone going blank for a split second, which most of us can't even dream about. It's almost verboten. A nightmarish existence. Without thought.

Mark knows that he hasn't practiced writing enough, because it's always felt like work. He's fully aware of what he's up to. Maybe all writers do. He's never heard an author say: "That short story felt like nothing. I can't even remember writing it." It's always all this work that went into it. You can't be blank while you write. Maybe that's why he's practicing here. Maybe it's all practice. For what? For when? Just tell Mark where to go, and he'll go blank; he'll empty out; he'll feel; he'll grieve. Just tell him where he should go. Show him the event again. He'll know not to think. It'll be like nothing this time. He's promising.

HOW I IMAGINE THINGS THAT I SO VAGUELY KNOW ABOUT

[44 YEARS BEFORE]

Lee wakes up in his dorm room during the first week of school at Springfield College and decides that he will get involved in extracurriculars. He puts on sneakers for this.

Volleyball? Tennis? Debate? Government? French club? Dance? Theater? Basketball? Football? Soccer? Lacrosse? Bands? Marching? Jazz? A capella groups? Track? Fraternities? Swimming? Weight lifting? Ping-Pong? Baseball? Ball at all? Religion? Church groups? Film club? Art? Literature? Book clubs? Chess? Newspaper? Outdoors club? Hiking? Camping? Fishing? Archery? Bows? Arrows? Guns? Culinary arts?

Lee has always been very hard working w/r/t his studies. He had looked around his Polish immigrant house, growing up. Saw his dad drinking, mostly. Saw his mom doing other people's laundry. Saw his older sister run off. And he knew to keep his nose down in order to get a view someday.

He chooses Track. One day. Heads off to the fields. Finds the coach with a whistle around his neck. Says he wants to try out. Runs a mile. Owns the record at Springfield College for some decades. Never competes.

Chooses Baseball. One day. Gets drafted to a minor league team. Never accepts offer.

But what was really happening? Really going on in Lee's days? In Lee's mind during any of this? How did he feel? He had 44 years to go. 44 years to choose or not choose. 44 years to live. 44 years to think and feel. How did he feel? It's the curiosity that lasts, not the sadness. I want to know. I want to ask. What was he thinking then? Back then before he became what we knew for such a short time. I want to ask him now. So much. What would he make of what's going on in the world now? Of me?

You know as well as I do. You tell me.

TENNIS

[IN REALITY]

I don't even really like tennis. Only half liked it when I played with any regularity. My eyesight has hindered my abilities on the court. The ball so small. So fast. You need detailed, responsive vision. You can't rely on peripheral vision, which is all I got. I don't want to play tennis. I'd rather play basketball, with its big flaming orange orb, impossible to miss, traveling at moderate speeds. The glorious orange hoop, the big white square on the enormous backboard. The lines on the court as long as ten men, as wide as a footprint. Much better.

I was never that good at tennis. Even practicing it is difficult. But my dad fucking died playing it! It's got to be the thing. Got to be. I've infused it with so much meaning and love that I can't play it anymore. It is my phobia, something else I share with my brother. Before playing, I hesitate: Is it safe?

GRAVE VISITS

[ELEVEN YEARS AFTER]

My mother and I are at the flower shop in Canton Center. We are looking at daisies. Daisies made up my mother's wedding bouquet. My dad used to get my mother daisies. I am going to name my first girl Daisy. We are there for daisies.

"Daisies, please," my mother says to the woman.

The woman disappears for a moment. My mother touches an orchid. "Isn't this lovely?" she asks me.

"Amazing," I say.

"How's this?" asks the woman with a bunch of daisies in her grasp.

"Great," says my mom.

"Great," I say. "Perfect."

The woman puts the daisies on the counter. She brandishes sheers. "How long would you like them?"

We both hesitate, trying to estimate the size of the grave's built-in vase.

"You're going to the cemetery," the woman says. She says it not with compassion, not as a question, not mean, not hurried. She just says it. She's saying: this happens all the time. This is life. I have no judgment. I have just this to ask, to say really, because I see that you are clearly going and don't know how to answer my question.

"Yes," says my mother.

We walk up the gentle slope of grass to his plaque in the ground. We wipe away cut grass. We look down at it. Mom asks for the bottle of water that I retrieved from the cemetery's supply by the offices. I hand it over. She pours the whole thing over the daisies in the built-in vase.

We look down at it.

"Oh, they look so nice," says my mother.

"They do," I say.

Time passes. Things. Stuff. We're practiced at this moment. We're good at it.

"Eleven years," says my mother.

"Eleven years," I say.

"It's over."

"We're out."

"I'm so happy to be out of it."

"We really are."

"We made it. Remember? Remember when we weren't?"

"Oh. I'm so happy we're out of it. It was a nightmare."

"The Nightmare Ages," I say.

"It's over."

"We made it, Mom."

THE NIGHTMARE AGES

[RECURRING WITHIN THE
FIRST COUPLE YEARS AFTER]

We don't talk about the Nightmare Ages. We remember them, with shudders and cringes, in flashes. Images. Sounds. Feelings. They come to us now, thankfully, less and less frequently. We were asleep during the Nightmare Ages. For years.

A rough cut in an otherwise ordinary dream of having breakfast on a warm weekend morning, staring out to the backyard. A nightmare cut to the sound of a spoon hitting the linoleum and something banging into the tabletop. David's elbows. Milk on the floor. The spoon clanging to a rest. David's eyes jammed into the heel of his palm, grunting out cries, whispering, "Fuck, fuck, fuck."

We don't talk about this Age. The Age when during a dream of an ordinary school day, walking the halls from English class to lunch, backpack heavy on the young back, there's a rough cut to Mark swiftly turning around, marching, all of a sudden, hiding his red face, staring down at his dress shoes and picking up speed, rushing to his car in the parking lot of the high school to climb inside, press his face to the backseat and wail in some sort of privacy, slamming a fist into cushions, calling out, "No, no, no."

We remember these nightmares, alone, and we flinch, while driving to the supermarket or the bar or the office, while waiting in line at the coffee shop, while watching a movie at home at night. We flinch and gasp at these sudden flashbacks. In the Nightmare Ages, the dream would cut without warning from watching the US Open on television to the sounds of a broken yell, and then just sobbing coming from Dad's old office room at the house. Mom sitting in Dad's old desk chair, trying to get papers in order, the business of the family's life, trying to figure out how to manage all the things Dad managed, hunched over folders inside cabinets, papers scattered everywhere over the tile. Mom crushing a document to her scrunched face, crying, "Oh goddammit, goddammit, oh god."

We saw all this. We heard it. We felt it. We were there. But they stopped happening so frequently, so desperately, so violently. We recall them, when we aren't expecting to, and we shake our limbs and heads, slap and wipe at our chests and faces to get the Nightmare Ages off us now, like cobwebs. We're happy to realize now, it was all only a bad dream. We woke up. They are almost all cleaned off now. The Nightmare Ages.

TUESDAY AFTERNOON

Two photos of my father. One framed, on my desk. One in a plastic sleeve in a drawer.

I pick up the framed photo. It shows my father in a blue Izod tennis shirt from sternum up. He's holding both my brother and me. I'm real young, too young to remember this moment. My brother is, as he's always been and will always be, six and a half years older, more a developed person. My brother's hair is so blond it's almost white, with great spools of thick curls all over the place. My hair is dirty blond and straight, in a bowl cut. My father is looking right at me, here in my apartment. He's looking directly into the lens, there in our front yard. My brother and I look more curious about the camera than cognizant that this split second in time will last, will stay with me, tangible and forever away. My father's look. I'll never write it right, but it has every single one of his expressions in one. His eyes say he is stable, to be counted on, a solid man, but not stern. The left side of his mouth, from my perspective, here in the apartment, not in the reality of the split second, says he is smiling, but he is not about to laugh by any means; he is happy but respectful of how this moment will remain, respectful maybe of preservation. The right side of his mouth says he is going to protect my mother and brother and me, with its proximity to the scar on his chin, which he got I-don't-know-how-or-when but probably protecting us. The lines on his forehead say he may need a nap after all this carrying us around all the time. But, then, his eyes, again, at another glance say he's laughing, say he's bursting on the inside with foolish love for us. His eyes, again, at another glance, say he must be going now. They say goodbye sometimes. He may know that he has to leave for work. They may say he has to leave for a tennis match. They may say he has to leave for good. For bad. For weird. Forever.

The photo in the plastic sleeve is nearly a candid, though he is looking at the camera. My dad's in green O.R. scrubs with a green O.R. mask tied over his mouth and nose. He has a green O.R. kerchief wrapped over his head. He is wielding a syringe, hovering over a patient, below white globes of light, about to put someone to sleep and keep him or her alive during an operation. He is in Ecuador, volunteering in the wilderness. His eyes say exactly the same thing.

This is all they ever say.

No matter where I'm looking.

I'll protect you all.

I must be going.

This is no lie.

I replace the photos and reach for my wallet, keys, and bag. I'm off to a million other things. The concerns of my day. Do I remember any of this when I'm rushing to a train? When I'm bumming a smoke? Does this matter when I'm asking you the time on the street corner? Buying milk or eggs? Do I remember? Is it real all the time? Am I unsure usually? Sure I am.

OUR SECRET

[BEFORE AND UNTIL NOW]

My dad drove a beautiful silver Porsche until the day he died. My brother took the reigns after. But it was always 'Dad's car,' and I thought it was just the coolest thing ever.

His silver Porsche 944, unable to be inconspicuous, would pop up on the hill above the soccer fields where I practiced for my middle school and high school, on the dirt road leading to the diamonds of baseball practices. He wouldn't just watch the games. He came to the practices, sitting back in the Porsche watching me practice. I wonder what he got out of that. Practice is more important than the game.

So, my dad fractured his wrist this one time. I forget how. Maybe I'll ask my mom, if I really care to remember. But he had a cast on for a little while. He still drove to work in his silver Porsche, shifting somehow with the cast on his right arm and hand. It must've been a struggle, because when he picked me up from practices, he would ask if I wanted to do the shifting, if I would put the car in gear. I was stoked to do this. He would say: "First!" then "Second" and so on. Until eventually, I was shifting at the appropriate times without his commands. I listened to the engine. It wasn't hard to tell when he was depressing the clutch—the engine would cease its growling—and I threw the gear shift into fifth.

We rode like this. Thinking back, it seems more than a little dangerous. I was not old enough to drive during these episodes. If I had mistakenly thrown the car into reverse, for instance, while leaving a stop light? Well!

But I never did botch this task. I was good at it. Really good. And when my dad's arm healed and the cast came off, I would still ask to shift for him, until that was the norm. He'd pick me up, or we'd pull out of the garage, and I would take the gearshift.

On the way to Martha's Vineyard, just my father and me, on Rte. 28, the highway that cuts down the cape, over the Bourne Bridge, and leads you to vessels that carry you to islands, my father and I spotted a red sports car zoom past us, speeding furiously. But the red car didn't keep speeding: it zoomed past, then slowed when it was just about to leave our sight. It waited for us to catch up. When we were parallel with this red sports car, the driver kept perfect pace in order to look over at us, to get our attention. My dad waved to them. I stared, felt nervous. They were two older guys, in their twenties I'd guess now, and they shouted something we couldn't hear through their closed windows and ours. What was going on here? Were we in trouble? Were these men police officers? FBI? Were they mad at my father for a careless move on the highway and wanted to fight? They stopped shouting. Zoomed away again. Slowed, came parallel again. Shouted more.

What happens next is the dumbest, most irresponsible, and greatest thing my father ever did, and I was told to keep it secret. At least until we were a safe distance from the event. Maybe now. Now that he's gone away.

My dad floated his silver Porsche 944 over to the far left lane. He accelerated. We were going sixty, seventy, my father told me to shift it to fourth. Fourth? We were going as fast as possible already in fifth. But I obeyed, and when I counter-intuitively downshifted, my father let go the clutch, and the gears inside the beautiful machine caught, the silver car shot forward as if by after burners, pinning me to my seat. The needle hovered around ninety miles per hour. My father put his arm out in front of me and slowed the car, floated it over to the far right lane, getting us back down to speed limit. I heard the engine stop roaring and shifted it back into fifth, resting the metal animal.

So, my father had put me in danger by driving so fast, just to get away from these guys in their red sports car. Who knows what they wanted.

But the red car zoomed past us again, until nearly out of sight, and they began to slow.

My father floated our silver animal over to the passing lane, pushed down the accelerator. We gained on them, the needle pushing eighty. I threw the beast into fourth as we came parallel with them, when I heard the car's heart skip a beat. I pulled down on the gearshift. Catapulted up the highway, other cars standing still. When the power boost of the high-speed downshift had leveled out, I put the animal in fifth again. My father was not talking with me. He didn't need to anymore. We were working together to fly this silver craft to its full potential. The red car appeared in the rearview mirror, and my father accelerated. A bend in the highway, the Bourne bridge coming into view, that high shining bridge, that gateway. It loomed, and we sped, my father changing lanes to avoid the frozen cars. The needle pushed 100, and I felt amazing. I felt like an explorer, like a space man, like my dad. Had we wings, we would be aloft. In our secret irresponsibility. The red car remained in the rearview. The needle climbed, 110, 115, 120, 125. We were moving at 130 miles per hour. The red car was gone from the rearview, probably now parked and just admiring us through binoculars. A small crowd gathering to watch this unprecedented feat.

The scream of a silver Porsche's engine at 140 miles per hour prohibits conversation: it demands you listen to it alone. It conveys so much power, so much energy, precision and heart that you submit, revere, and allow the sound to grow, become more than sound, a being. Pressed against the seat, the road and cars and trees and grass and clouds and suns whipping by in a missile Monet, I looked to my father, who looked to me for just one split second. The big shining bridge charged toward us, the highway would narrow to two lanes, without dividers, we would eventually be two hundred feet above the Cape Cod canal, forced to come down slow.

I listened to the engine. I left my hand on the shifter. My father pressed the gas, and I'm sure that our little silver blur rocketed so fast that when we hit the bridge, we flew clean to the beaches of Martha's Vineyard. Everything got hotter, louder. This symbiosis that my dad and I had managed with this silver rocket! Smiles. We went so fast that everything went white. We vanished. Went away. Sailed beyond. Created an energy together that moved us into another dimension. Another zone, where we could remain forever together. Moving so fast. Floating. Flying. Into fiction.

TENNIS WITH HEAVEN GRAVITY

[ONGOING AFTER]

There are times when—walking down the block from his apartment to the corner store for a pack of cigarettes or to the subway stop after work or pacing around a waiting room—even though it's been years since he's played, Mark tosses an invisible ball into the air and strikes it with an invisible racquet. This is always performed in slow motion, or with moon gravity, or (if he wants to be sentimental, and he does at the moment) this is performed with heaven-gravity. Everything floats. It's all invisible. Everything works out flawlessly. The ball rises to its peak; knees bend; muscles ready themselves for uncoiling; left hand points to the ball; right hand launches up, slowly, to make contact. The perfect serve. And he feels the ball hit the strings of the invisible racquet. The sensation begins in his palm, cascades down his forearm and settles in his chest. This warms Mark for a second when it's cold out. It distracts him when he's sad or nervous. Just quick. Sometimes, instead of a serve, it's a slow motion, heaven-gravity forehand where he feels the contact and rolls his wrist over the ball, top spin. * Pop * It's always an inside out forehand to an invisible ad court. It's always a winner. An impossible angle. Heaven geometry. And Mark thinks he's returning his dad's last serve, the one that maybe made it over the net when he exploded. Mark can't help but feel a smile beginning behind his jaw and his eyes in the act of these invisible ghost shots. His body just does this. Sometimes he laughs. He always continues on with the concerns of his day.

209

TUESDAY EVENING

I have triangulated, strained, and listened for my train's track. I have heard. I have run. I have got myself a window. I have given over my ticket. The sun has dipped itself half down below the horizon. I have stared out the window at the row homes of Dorchester, the empty lots of Hyde Park.

The sun sets, and I can see a blurry reflection of my face in the window. People say that I look just like my father. My brother says I look as if our dad had asexually reproduced a son. I see him in my face, when the mirror's dirty, fucked up, like this makeshift one here. I think about what it would be like to be sixteen or seventeen, attending a bereavement group meeting at which I knew there was to be a guest speaker, a twenty-something, who had gone through the same thing that I am currently going through. How would I feel about him, about the meeting? I remember ex-drug addicts coming to speak with us kids at school. They went through it for us, so we don't have to. Their names are all gone. Their speeches were mocked after the assembly. Their stories recounted in jest. Their help of no help. This is what I am about to become. A nameless mockable man, come out of the ether to share bullshit stories that are supposed to be affecting but are not. I'm relieved that I at least tossed the outline and handouts and the rest. I think about sitting there, in a community center conference room or church basement and wanting nothing but to be long gone from there. These kids don't want to be there, and I want to be on their side. They are probably forced to attend, and they think it's bullshit. It is bullshit. The grown-ups don't have it right. I'm now a grown-up to them, to that younger version of me.

How could I get my younger me to believe that this older me is not the human manifestation of a bull's shit? I care for that younger me. I am sad for him.

Brutal honesty is what I land on as the train lands at the Rte. 128 station in Canton. Brutal fucking honesty. I have something to say, something honest. None of that bullshit. No one will forget this little speech.

"I'm still upset," I tell my mother as we drive in her black Ford Explorer over to Foxboro, the town in which this meeting is to occur, I now learn. In a Foxboro community center. Not a church.

"It will be fine," my mother assures me.

I am unpredictably happy during the drive. It is like an outing with my mother. It is like we are spending time together, as if this makes up for all the times she mentioned museum exhibitions, open studios, plays downtown, lunch, or some other get-together that I said yes to and then simply waited for the date to pass. I feel as though we are finally doing something together. Our outing. It feels not a lot like work, but it gives me a sense of duty soon to be accomplished. I feel good to have finally shown up for her.

"Do you have any more intel on this?"

"No. I know that Kathy runs the meetings."

"Who is Kathy?"

"I told you—"

"Just agree that you've told me nothing."

"I told you: Kathy is Suzanne's friend, and she lost her husband and has started this group, and now all these women who have lost their husbands attend with their kids who have all lost their dads. And it's not just for kids who have lost dads. It just so happens that that's who attends."

"Gotcha."

The white linoleum, the white walls, the white ceiling, the white counter tops, the white tables, the white chairs, the white doors, the white window shades, and the white fluorescent lights make entering the community center's conference room look like *you know what.*

I understand that everyone I'm looking at lives with a dead person. The high school girl, who looks perfectly normal, who has even brought her white puppy with her, she lives with a dead dad. The tiny elementary school kid with his white toy car, playing on the white floor, he plays with a dead dad. The three women drinking cups of tea, talking softly with each other in the white chairs around the white table, they sleep with dead husbands. The middle school kid with the hood of his sweatshirt up over his head, who is playing a Beethoven tune on the piano, his dad died recently and he practices piano with a dead dad. The woman offering me coffee or tea in a white mug, holding a white kettle and pointing to a white coffee maker, she makes tea at home for a husband who died. The woman I enter with, my mother, wearing a jacket that belonged to my dad, who is shaking hands and smiling and meeting and greeting the other women and petting the girl's dog, her husband, one night, ten years ago, exploded on a tennis court, and here she is.

I take a white mug, pour in milk from a white carton. I sit in a white chair, lean on the white table, look for a second at the white light and white piano and white dog and white refrigerator and white packets of sugar. I smile at everybody. I shake hands, introduce myself. I wait for I don't know what to happen.

Then the I don't know what begins.

"Everyone, we have two new people joining us tonight: Henrietta and Mark, who are seated right here." This is Kathy talking. She indicates my mother and me. The two of us, I imagine we look like celebrities at a tennis match or Celtics game, the camera pointing us out, unmiked, waving, waiting to be left alone again. I mouth a *hello,* and I don't know why. "So, welcome," Kathy says. "Amy," Kathy says to a woman holding a clipboard. "Do you want to take the kids into the other room?"

I assume it is Amy who agrees to this, and all the young people stand up and follow Amy. I remain seated. Amy waves me a 'come on.' Kathy says, "Why don't you join them, Mark." The two factions are separating. The dead-dad-kids to one room, the dead-husband-women remain in this one. I look to my mother, and I say, I will see you later, I guess. I leave her, and it feels like we are being separated into different rooms for detention. I don't turn around. I just leave with the kids.

We enter through another white door into a smaller white room with more white chairs and white tables and white walls and white cupboards and white floors and stacks of blank white paper and white pencils, there are plastic white forks, knives, spoons, plates, bowls, napkins; white coat hooks and a white clock.

We take our seats around a table. I lean back, finger my mug of coffee, try to appear relaxed, hoping that going through the physical motions of relaxedness will coax the emotional ones into action. I relaxedly ask the girl her dog's name, age, breed. She answers. I immediately can't remember.

The white door closes, comes flush to the white wall and white ceiling and white floor. Suddenly, there is no depth to anything in this white world.

It is dawning on me that I am coming up to a point in time when I will have lived consciously longer with the death of my father than I have lived with my father. Childhood memories are treasures and all that, but when do we fully start to comprehend our surroundings? At five? At eight? Those years? Can we declare that we lived those years with full consciousness? I am not sure. Every period of my life has been followed by a period in which I look back on my earlier self as childish, with real curiosity about the younger me's decisions; I am still forming. I don't even think of two-years-ago-me as related to present-me. Maybe we do this forever. But I believe that I became fully conscious a little while after my father died. Everything up until his death seems different. Before. Everything following directly after, a weird and bad dream. Everything after some unknown point, after: conscious life. So, if I were fully conscious and able to comprehend life at seven years old, then I am, right now, at the point when half my life has been with him and half without. I feel I have had a more meaningful relationship with the dead man than I did with the living man. All the events of my life, even the ones before he died, in memory, are now and will forever be events that I have shared with a death, not a person.

Scene 1

When I walked into the white room with the fatherless kids at the bereavement group meeting, I saw my father. He was waiting for us to enter the room. He was standing by the white table with the white coffee cups on it. He was in his green O.R. scrubs with his green O.R. mask over his mouth and nose, but it was him. He leaned back on the table and it gave a little, so he stood straight up and folded his arms.

"Dad?"

"Mark?"

"What are you doing here?"

"What are you doing here?"

"Mom made me come to talk to these kids about losing you."

"Hmm."

"And you?"

"I am lost."

"Lost?"

"You lost me. I am a little confused, son."

"You're telling me."

"Well, I don't think you should be talking to these kids, considering."

"Considering the fact that you are here? You're always here. But you've always got to get going. You must be leaving."

"Yes. But how do you explain this?" He unfolded his arms and indicated his standing plainly on the white linoleum.

"Then let's get out of here."

My father then saw the group of kids behind me, entering the room. "Excuse me, sorry," he said to the lot of them. "There's been a misunderstanding."

"My dad's here," I told the group. "I'm really sorry. I can't talk with you now."

"Fuck," said one of the kids.

"Well, I wish we had known that," said the woman with the clipboard.

"I'm really sorry," I told her.

"We'll just get going," my dad told her, and he and I padded back to the room to fetch my mother.

"Mom!" I shouted, interrupting. "Look what the cat dragged in!"

Then my dad strode into the room with his O.R. scrubs, pulled down his O.R. mask, and said: "Hank!"

My mom stood up. "What?"

"There's no need to be here anymore," I told her.

"Oh," she said, and looked a little embarrassed. "I'm sorry," she told the other women in the room. "My husband's been here all along. What a mix up!"

"Well, good luck with that," said one of the women.

Then we were grabbing our coats, rushing, apologizing to the group, and getting into my mom's black Ford Explorer. Me in the back. Mom in the passenger seat. My dad at the wheel as it had always been.

"I can't wait to get home and call Dave and tell him the news!" my mom squealed.

"Where to?" my dad asked us before putting the truck in gear.

"Home?" I suggested.

"Sure," said my mom.

"Home it is then," my dad said and put it in drive.

We rode back, me looking out the window. My mom putting in a CD. My dad dangling his arm out the window.

Then I said, "close call on giving that little talk to those kids. Dodged that one just in time."

Everyone laughed.

It seemed impossible. But granted this reprieve, none of us looked in the rearview mirror.

God, we were excited.

Scene 2

No.

What really happened:

The white room had a window on the far wall with white blinds drawn and a white pull string dangling before it. We gathered around the table and sat, all of us, at the same instant with the same grace. I squeezed my white coffee cup and asked the girl next to me the name of her white dog, the breed, and the age but couldn't register what she told me. The sipping of the coffee, the chitchat: I attempted to coax the emotional state of relaxedness into being through outward physical expressions of comfort. It had not yet worked.

A pitter-patting started up, and I thought it was in my head, or that my body was preparing itself for a kind of ridiculous primitive battle, conjuring adrenaline, hormones, and maxing out my senses, allowing me to hear the clicking electricity of the white refrigerator with now heightened perception.

"What's that?" asked a boy with long blond hair, turning in the direction of the window.

"Rain," said the woman with the clipboard.

"I don't think so," I said and shocked myself with the immediate authority.

"That really doesn't sound like rain," said the blond boy.

"That's rain. That's rain and that's an ok thing," said the lady with the clipboard.

"No," I said. "Fuck." My ears hurt. I stood, knocking over my chair, walked to the white window, pulled on the white string, and lifted the white blinds.

It was dark out in the parking lot that wrapped around the entire community center, but it was clear what the *pitter-patting* then

drumming then *roaring* had been. A steady downpour of green
PENN tennis balls, thundering down on our cars and the pavement
and the puddles. When they crashed down, they exploded, popped.
Pop. Pop. POP-POP-POP!!! The tennis balls popped and splashed
in green puddles and tiny explosions of green ran in streams, joined
in pools and steadily rose.

"Not rain," said the blond boy.

"My mistake," said the woman with the clipboard.

"Well, it will probably pass over soon enough," I said and motioned
for us to head back to the table and gather ourselves for the discussion.
I picked up my chair and scooted into position.

"Well," said the woman with the clipboard, "Mark is joining us
tonight, and I would like to offer him the chance to tell us his story."

The drumming and splashing and popping PENN tennis balls
cut out. The silence, the noticing of that great noise ceasing, the new
quiet, it made us all that much more aware of what had been going
on just one second ago—we immediately missed the thunder.

And I began.

Scene 3

No.

So I began the telling. Began the story for all of them, all who had
lost. "One night, my father exploded—"

But then, I saw that a punk kid, skinny as anything, with hair falling
in front of his face, Strike, now sat where the blond boy had been.
He was doodling in a spiral-bound notebook with his left hand and
reaching for his backpack at his feet with his right. It took one second
for his boney hand with black-painted nails to vanish into the first
zippered compartment then reappear with a silver pistol, cocked. He
stood, and we all put our hands up.

Another kid, his mother, and three of his friends, Carl and Lester
and Laura, crawled out from under the table and unlatched a
thirteen-rung ladder, setting up a grand stunt. Mountains fluttered
into view in the distance, beyond the white room.

"Wait," I shouted to them. "Just wait!" I rose cautiously from my chair. They focused their eyes on me. It was my fault, and I needed to protect the woman with the clipboard and all the real kids from this deadly situation.

I floated one of my hands over the crowd, telling the punk that he didn't need to hurt them, that they didn't need any more pain, did they? But then Harmony and Gertrude, holding brown grocery bags, pulled up chairs around the white table. The two of them waited, eyes on me, expecting. Garewood materialized, over by the sink, notebook tucked under his arm, he stared right at me. Anna, struggling with a box labeled "Kitchen Plates," stared me down, sticking her tongue into her cheek, demanding I say something, back by the windows with drawn white blinds. Daniel and Dean and Devon, all of them the same person at different stages of life, all of them my brother, they all appeared around the white table, holding an axe, a camera, and a refill of napkins, wearing *I told you so* on their faces. Matt and Max and Manny and Mason and Marshall stepped out from within me, walked out of my body as if through a wormhole, giving me the chills. They flipped me the bird, shot me a sarcastic OK symbol, offered a cynical thumbs up, and drew a pointer finger across their necks. They took their seats in the chairs around the white table with the rest of them. More streamed in through the white walls—Holty and Flower carrying their new baby and glaring at me as they found their seats; a foursome of men in tennis whites, tennis racquets propped on shoulders, looking pissed at me; the ghost of Charles Lin with an armload of envelopes to mail, snarling; Michael and the Professor quieting their argument to focus on me; Douglas and Martin waving tennis racquets, looking for empty chairs; another Lester dusting off his overalls; another Carl, bleary-eyed, spinning a basketball on his middle finger—they all quieted and folded their hands on the table and waited, gesturing for me to sit, as well, gesturing to me that they were waiting, *we're waiting, we're all here. Don't you have something to say? You always have something for us to say... Will you stop using fiction? Will you find the courage to own your truth on the matter? Can you, here, now, when it counts, say something of your own? Can you step up and say one honest thing for us? The only thing of substance and originality you can possibly offer anyone is your own very personal feelings on this matter. So do you know? Will you share it? What happened? Tell us.*

The room was packed with the real and the unreal. The gun in the punk's hand turned to steam, and he shot me a look, stunned. I reached into my pants pocket and withdrew a crumpled pen pal note: "*How do you feel, asshole? Write back, asshole...*"

I have read and believe that everyone in your dreams is yourself. Every word spoken in a dream by someone: you are the one saying it. Everything that you see someone else doing: you are the one doing it. Everything you intuit someone else feeling: you are the one feeling it. You are the only one there. It makes sense.

I have also read and believe that when you begin to describe something, to write down how it looked or felt or sounded, you lose some of the memory. If you live it, then write it down, what you've written takes over your memory. Your writing becomes the memory if you write too much of it. Describe his face, and you lose the memory of his face. Describe the feeling, and you lose the feeling. Whatever you write becomes the new truth. What you write becomes all you've got.

"So." Amy gathers all our attentions with a word. She shuffles blank sheets of white paper. "Mark, would you tell us your story?"

Story? Is it a story? A memory? A memoir? Shouldn't she be asking for my Personal Essay? A short piece of creative nonfiction?

She asked for my *story*.

all are weird manifestations of himself, coming to confront him

A MOMENT OF REFLECTION

[AS CONTEMPORARY AS THIS GETS]

I have never written a personal essay, a piece of nonfiction. I have no idea how it's done. I've heard that it involves exposition, the telling instead of the showing, something that fiction writers are not supposed to do. Again, though, these rules aren't really rules; they're sound bites to get through a workshop, give out a critique. I'm not used to telling. Not in fiction or real life. I see that now. If I'm going to get anywhere in fiction, I have got to put an end to this real life intrusion. To get anywhere in real life: the reverse. I've tried to write the story of what happened to my dad, my mom, my brother, and me when my dad died, in so many ways—in fiction—that the obviousness of what I need to do to progress has finally struck. I can't get any further in real life by using fiction. I can't get any further in fiction by using this real life trauma that is begging for a different kind of attention.

There was a long time when I ran from the truth, didn't want anyone to know, for this wrong reason or that. But I'm not scared of my dad's death anymore. Not scared of what it will make me look like. Not scared that talking about it will somehow corrupt my emotions about it all. Not scared of feeling something and expressing it. Because I'm out of fiction about it. The inkwell's dry. I know how to free myself. I know I want to be freed.

The editors at the press that is publishing this book suggested there be a moment of reflection before the ending. In nonfiction, people expect those passages of reflection, some good old exposition, they told me.

I think they're right. That probably does belong here. It was my fault that it wasn't here already, not more of a presence throughout the book, those expository insights. Here I am, though, at thirty-four years old, looking back on something I wrote at twenty-nine, searching for how to add that moment of reflection. Of course, I couldn't see it then, but I do now. It took me this long.

But I hesitate to take this suggestion. Not because I think it is incorrect, that it won't benefit. I hesitate because this book is an artifact. It's a preserved document under glass. It's a desperate and scattered and sad young man frozen in a block of ice. It's a fossil I've just extracted from the drawer, dusting at the bones with the archaeologist's brush, carefully lifting it out of the earth heaped on it, deep within the desk. If I add too much of my perspective from where I sit now, it will crack.

Since completing this thing about my dad's death and my avoiding dealing with it in real life, preferring to hide my feelings and obsessions in fiction, I haven't written about this stuff—death, grief, loss. All that, it's been over with for years.

After attending the bereavement group and then writing this nonfictional overlay about the week leading up to it, I have never felt inclined to touch this subject. I now talk about my dad's death and its effects with real people in my life. I now write fiction devoid of lingering wounds that tend to fuck it all up anyhow. This thing you've read, it freed me.

Is exposition telling the reader what the writer thinks is the meaning ort theme of a work? My impulse is to just come right out and tell you: in this book fiction interrupts real life; the real stuff rams itself into the fiction. The two intertwine the way it seemed to in my experiences. The death of my father kept popping up in my stories, stories that didn't want anything to do with him or his death. Fiction kept popping up in the real stuff —when I would protect myself by imagining what real things could mean in fiction, become in a story. That's what was going on in here.

Sections of this book contain commentary on short stories, giving my insights and analysis with the perspective of years of distance. Now

I have that distance on the whole book. What I see is a kid making a last ditch effort to throw everything—about this major complication in his life and fiction—down on the page, then toss everything up into outer space, everything that wouldn't stop demanding to be seen, heard, felt. It worked. I now see that it worked. I see someone living half in his head, fictionalizing, half in reality. It was just too weird to keep living like that. I tossed it all up. It all vanished.

Thank you for letting me. I hope it wasn't as confusing for you as it was for me. I hope it wasn't too long, either; you have your own stuff going on.

Real expressions of feeling about losing my dad at seventeen lie no longer in a book.

Onward.

TUESDAY EVENING

So what did I say to the room full up of these unreal characters?

I said: "I'm sorry that I used you. I am sorry for what I've done to you. But thank you." I put each one of the characters directly in the center of my field of vision, right in the center of my dead fovea cells, and each ghostly character vanished.

And what did I say to the room of dead-dad-having kids?

"I have my story about the death of someone I love, which is not like your story at all. But, here it is anyway: One night, my father went off to play tennis with his friends, just as he had done the previous week, just as he had always done. I never saw him again."

ACKNOWLEDGMENTS

I wouldn't have written this or anything else if my brother Dave didn't make reading really interesting stuff and writing fiction seem like the coolest thing in the world. Way back when, I did whatever you did, because I basically wanted to be just like you, and right at the right time you were writing stories and screenplays and plays and reading the hippest stuff around. Thank you for opening all this up to me! And, of course, Dave wouldn't have been able to make anything seem awesome, if our Ma Henrietta hadn't kept us alive and raised us and made us safe and allowed us to pursue our interests, feeling like we could actually do whatever we dedicated ourselves to. And, to get away from the philosophical and zenish, I couldn't have written fiction and studied it and worked at it like I have if it wasn't for my Ma giving me so much support throughout so much of my young-to-not-so-young young adult life—housing, food, money, love, encouragement. You really kept everything together after it all went down, Ma. Thank you! But interest in writing and general life support only go so far, so there are many teachers-turned-friends who I owe so much, namely: Vicky Seelen for making a teenager think that pursuing fiction writing was a sincere and good thing; Greg Hrbek for the years of advice, critique, friendship, and support and for showing me what it means to really do this stuff; Kathryn Davis for above and beyond professional help, encouragement, advice, and friendship and inspiring fiction; Elizabeth Evans for tricking me into thinking I had talent and continuing to support my work through the years; and Jonathan Penner, Jason Brown, and Aurelie Sheehan for giving me so much advice that I think back on all the time. And what can you do, really, without great friends deluding you into thinking you're actually good at something: Will!, thank you for being so excited about my stuff and always telling me it's good and funny and creative; Rich!, thank you for helping me through the darkest of times, brother, and for always reading my stories out loud, even when your throat hurt! John!, thank you for taking my writing seriously, for doing close reads, for talking with me at length about this stuff, for your sincerity and honesty, and for your work as commissioner; Gavin!, thank you for supporting this avid indoorsman; William, Donald, and Lisa!, thank you for reading this book in its earliest iterations way back, and for always being there to talk writing, read stuff, and, of course, for all the support! Jamie and Cara!, for all the advice, all the great feedback, all the conversations and friendship! Tim Denevi, who had nothing and everything to do with the publication of this book, thank you for introducing me to Stillhouse. And the Stillhouse folks, Marcos, Justin, Meghan, and Seth, who put so much work into this book to make it better, thank you for caring. And then there were three: Rachel Yoder: thank you, friend, for always reading my stories aloud in class when I couldn't see well enough to do so, for so, so much of my formative conversations about writing fiction, for being my confessor and friend and advisor and everything, for making the magazine with me, for your friendship. Steven Millhauser!, thank you for turning a 21 year-old boy interested in writing into a 34 year-old boy who understands how to be serious about writing: no one has had more influence on my writing, this is all largely your doing. And, lastly but certainly not leastly, Alle!, you give me more love, more fanatical support, and more inspiration than I ever thought I deserved, thank you for our life together.

ABOUT THE AUTHOR

Mark Polanzak's prose has appeared in such places as *The Adirondack Review*, *Gingko Tree Review*, *Pindeldyboz*, *Third Coast*, *The Pinch*, *The Southern Review*, *Wag's Revue*, and *The American Scholar*, among others. His story "A Proper Hunger" won second place in the Italo Calvino Prize for Fabulist Fiction. He received his MFA from the University of Arizona. In addition to writing, Polanzak is also a founding editor of *draft: the journal of process*. He teaches writing at the Berklee College of Music in Boston.

www.draftjournal.com

This book would not have been possible without
the hard work of our staff.

We would like to acknowledge:

Justin Lafreniere & Marcos L. Martínez, Managing Editors

Marcos L. Martínez, Editor-in-Chief
Meghan McNamara, Director of Media & Communications
Douglas J. Luman, Art Director
Scott W. Berg, Editorial Advisor

stillhouse press

Editors

Matt Christovich
Todd Covalcine
Douglas J. Luman
Meghan McNamara
Suzy Rigdon
Merrill Sunderland
Qinglan Wang

Editorial Interns

Hannah Campeanu
Madeline Dell'Aria
Ah-reum Han
Benjamin Rader
Katie Ray
Michelle Webber

Our Donors

Maziar Gahvari
Gerald Prout

CPSIA information can be obtained
at www.ICGtesting.com
Printed in the USA
LVOW12s0232260117

522225LV00003B/39/P

9 780990 516927